# THE ESSENTIAL GUIDE TO FACILITATING PROJECT MANAGEMENT WORKSHOPS

# THE
# ESSENTIAL GUIDE
## TO FACILITATING PROJECT
# MANAGEMENT
# WORKSHOPS

## LYNDA CARTER
### Illustrated by David Balan

Competitive Edge Consulting, Inc., Cleveland 44107
©2017 by Lynda Carter
Printed in the United States of America

ISBN: 978-0-9903549-3-2

Library of Congress Control Number: 2017913158

Edited by Brenda Judy
www.publishersplanet.com

Illustrated by David Balan
www.davidbalan.com

Cover and Interior Design by Carolyn Sheltraw
www.csheltraw.com

⊚ This paper meets the requirements of ANSI/NISO Z39.48-1992 (Permanence of Paper).

www.cectraining.com

To everyone who agrees that
two minds are better than one.

# Table of Contents

Acknowledgments. . . . . . . . . . . . . . . . . . . . . . . . . . . . . . . . ix

Introduction . . . . . . . . . . . . . . . . . . . . . . . . . . . . . . . . . . . xi

Workshop Overview. . . . . . . . . . . . . . . . . . . . . . . . . . . . . . 1
    The Value of Collaborative Workshops. . . . . . . . . . . . . . . . 3
    Workshop Framework . . . . . . . . . . . . . . . . . . . . . . . . . . . 5
    Workshop Roles and Responsibilities. . . . . . . . . . . . . . . . . . 7

Workshop Preparation . . . . . . . . . . . . . . . . . . . . . . . . . . . . 9
    Skills for the Workshop Facilitator. . . . . . . . . . . . . . . . . . . 11
    Defining the Workshop Purpose . . . . . . . . . . . . . . . . . . . . 15
    Identifying Workshop Participants. . . . . . . . . . . . . . . . . . . 17
        Workshop Preparation Roles and Responsibilities . . . . . . 18
    Creating the Workshop Agenda. . . . . . . . . . . . . . . . . . . . 21
        Planning Workshop . . . . . . . . . . . . . . . . . . . . . . . . . 22
        Closing Workshop . . . . . . . . . . . . . . . . . . . . . . . . . . 27
    Inviting Participants. . . . . . . . . . . . . . . . . . . . . . . . . . . 31
    Workshop Supplies . . . . . . . . . . . . . . . . . . . . . . . . . . . 35
    Finalizing Room Logistics . . . . . . . . . . . . . . . . . . . . . . . 37

Workshop Details. . . . . . . . . . . . . . . . . . . . . . . . . . . . . . . 39
    Workshop Details Overview . . . . . . . . . . . . . . . . . . . . . . 41
        Workshop Roles and Responsibilities . . . . . . . . . . . . . . 43
    Kick-Off . . . . . . . . . . . . . . . . . . . . . . . . . . . . . . . . . . 45
        Workshop Welcome . . . . . . . . . . . . . . . . . . . . . . . . . 45
        Sponsor Kick-off. . . . . . . . . . . . . . . . . . . . . . . . . . . 49
        Project Manager Kick-off . . . . . . . . . . . . . . . . . . . . . 52
    Project Management Techniques . . . . . . . . . . . . . . . . . . . 55

Clarifying the Project Goal . . . . . . . . . . . . . . . . . . . . . . 55
Gathering Lessons Learned from Previous Projects . . . . . 59
Analyzing Stakeholders and Their Key Performance
    Indicators (KPI) . . . . . . . . . . . . . . . . . . . . . . . . . . . . . 63
Defining Project Deliverables . . . . . . . . . . . . . . . . . . . . . 68
Defining Project Deliverables Acceptance
    Criteria/Requirements . . . . . . . . . . . . . . . . . . . . . . . . . 72
Developing the Project Time Line. . . . . . . . . . . . . . . . . . 75
Defining Project Roles and Responsibilities
    Using the RACI Chart . . . . . . . . . . . . . . . . . . . . . . . . . 79
Identifying, Assessing and Managing Project Risks . . . . . 83
Documenting Project Issues . . . . . . . . . . . . . . . . . . . . . . 90
Creating the Communication Plan . . . . . . . . . . . . . . . . . 93
Wrap-Up . . . . . . . . . . . . . . . . . . . . . . . . . . . . . . . . . . . . . . . . 99
Report Out. . . . . . . . . . . . . . . . . . . . . . . . . . . . . . . . . . . 99
Workshop Close Out . . . . . . . . . . . . . . . . . . . . . . . . . . 101

**Post Workshop** . . . . . . . . . . . . . . . . . . . . . . . . . . . . . . . . . . 103
Updating Documentation . . . . . . . . . . . . . . . . . . . . . . . 105
Completing Action Items. . . . . . . . . . . . . . . . . . . . . . . . 107
Post Workshop Roles and Responsibilities . . . . . . . . . . . 109
Resources for Supporting Workshops . . . . . . . . . . . . . . . 111

**Appendixes** . . . . . . . . . . . . . . . . . . . . . . . . . . . . . . . . . . . . . 113
Appendix A: Planning and Closing Forms . . . . . . . . . . . 115
Appendix B: Participant Invitations. . . . . . . . . . . . . . . . 121
Appendix C: Potential Slides . . . . . . . . . . . . . . . . . . . . . 125
Appendix D: Sample Workshop Output . . . . . . . . . . . . . 137

**Glossary** . . . . . . . . . . . . . . . . . . . . . . . . . . . . . . . . . . . . . . . 145

# Acknowledgments

Writing a book is truly a collaborative effort. The seed gets planted in conversations and grows until I sit down at the computer and the words flow.

The first draft is always a bit rough, so I want to take this opportunity to thank Gary Slavin, who inspires me to continue writing and is always willing to read a first draft.

To Carrie Brainerd, who spent many days observing, co-facilitating and leading planning workshops. Carrie took a red pen and enhanced this book's first draft.

To Brenda Judy, the official editor, who does more than edit, she asks questions that expand my understanding and provide improved structure and content for the final version of my books.

To Carolyn Sheltraw, who designed the book cover and turned my words and graphics into a presentable format.

I also want to thank those clients who have embraced collaborative planning and have willingly changed the way they plan. It has been my pleasure to see you grow and succeed.

# Introduction

The purpose of this book is to provide support for organizations and individuals who believe that the best planning is done when people come together to share their ideas. Specifically, this book explains how to design and run workshops for planning and closing out projects and programs. The result of each workshop is a series of whiteboards, brown paper, flip charts, sticky notes and spreadsheets that document a common approach for the project/program strategy. This book includes four sections:

- Workshop Overview – providing the value of a workshop, overview of a workshop, and an introduction to workshop roles and responsibilities
- Workshop Preparation – defining skills for the Facilitator, establishing the workshop purpose, creating the agenda, identifying and inviting participants,  gathering workshop supplies, and finalizing room logistics
- Workshop Details – detailing instructions for each workshop component (from kick-off to close-out), including purpose, outcome, supplies, potential slides used to facilitate the technique, timing, directions, alternatives and integration ideas
- Post Workshop – defining the action items to be completed after the workshop is over

This is a companion book to *The Practitioner's Guide to Project Management*. It serves as a basic facilitator's guide for creating immersion experiences in collaborative project planning. As you build your experience in group facilitation and applying project management techniques, draw on what you have learned to customize and enhance your workshops. When you come up with something new, let me know. We can all benefit from one another's experiences.

Experience is the greatest teacher. This is true for life, for work and for applying new skills like project management. So, create opportunities for yourself to practice, practice, practice.

# Section 1:
# WORKSHOP OVERVIEW

This section discusses the value of a workshop, overview of a workshop, and an introduction to workshop roles and responsibilities.

# The Value of Collaborative Workshops

Ever work on a project and wonder why major components were missed in planning? Maybe they were things that you knew about or other team members might have known about, had they been asked. When planning is the sole responsibility of the Project Manager, it can lead to under-scoping, under-estimating and overall under-planning.

We can't plan for things we don't know about. Vast though they may be, we are limited by our experiences. We need everyone's knowledge to develop a more thorough plan.

One-on-one conversations are helpful, but can leave an incomplete image of what project work needs to be completed. Getting everyone in the same room at the same time can be a difficult task. But once an organization sees the value of team planning, they rarely go back to the previous practice of planning as the sole activity of the Project Manager.

Management often sees project management as a training event, like checking the box off the to-do list. Once the training is done, the organization thinks it has mastered what is needed to deliver more organized and efficient projects. The truth is that project management is more a way of thought to approaching a problem than a list of techniques and forms and templates. Training helps, but training alone won't bring the value. Integrating project management into the organization requires the company to change the way it plans and staffs project work. A collaborative workshop is a great way to drive that change.

When an organization is serious about project management and wants to know how to reinforce the training, I recommend running planning workshops to get everyone immersed in real work and real applications. As I set up what is required for a workshop, I get resistance in the form of questions like: *"Why do so many people or departments need to be involved? Long meetings are never productive—does everyone need to be there the entire time?"* If there is enough leadership commitment to support one collaborative workshop, that is all it takes for the workshop to change the way people see planning. Most workshops start small, only a few representatives from key project areas. But as the workshop continues, workshop participants often call in others, saying, *"You need to get to this meeting; we need your experience to plan this project."* It's not unusual for more people to be invited into the workshop as the day progresses.

After walking through the outputs of a completed workshop with sponsors, I have had organizations decide that, in the future, no funds will be released for projects that do not run a collaborative planning workshop.

The benefits of collaborative planning include:

- Integrating different perspectives into one cohesive Project Plan
- A common vision for the entire Project Plan and project team
- Increased confidence in the accuracy of the Project Plan
- Application of best practices in project management

# Workshop Framework

Planning workshops can occur at any time in the life of a project. Workshops can be used in early planning to gather an overarching approach to achieve the project goals or any time during the project to create more clarity on a specific phase, deliverable or project component. Closing workshops can occur not only at the end of a project but at the end of a phase/stage or at key milestones to capture lessons learned and share with the team the actual value delivered by the project.

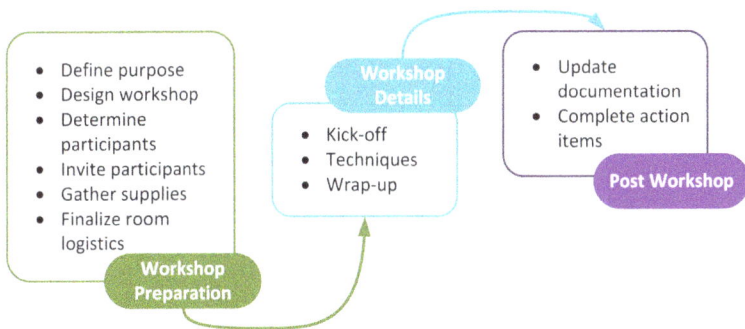

**Workshop Preparation**
- Define purpose
- Design workshop
- Determine participants
- Invite participants
- Gather supplies
- Finalize room logistics

**Workshop Details**
- Kick-off
- Techniques
- Wrap-up

**Post Workshop**
- Update documentation
- Complete action items

Workshops should be run like a mini-project. There is:

- *Initiation* to determine if a workshop makes sense and has leadership support
- *Planning* to complete the **workshop preparation** needed for success
- *Execution/Control and Monitoring* for running the **workshop details**
- *Closing* to complete the **post-workshop** activities

Each workshop is composed of three parts:

- Kick-off – The kick-off begins with the Project Sponsor sharing the business needs behind the project and how the project is aligned to the organization's strategy. The kick-off also introduces the workshop goals, outcomes, agenda, participants, project purpose and history, and how the workshop report out will be shared. The kick-off is led by both the Project Manager and the workshop Facilitator.
- Project Management Techniques – The Facilitator leads participants through applying the project management techniques to create portions of the Project Charter
- Wrap-up – The workshop ends when the project team identifies any open action items/next steps and then presents the workshop output to the Project Sponsor. The wrap-up is led by both the Project Manager and the workshop Facilitator.

# Workshop Roles and Responsibilities

There are multiple roles to be filled in a workshop. Each role is unique and requires different responsibilities. Here is a summary of the workshop roles and responsibilities:

| Icon | Role and Primary Responsibility |
|---|---|
| | The **Project Sponsor** is *or* represents the primary project benefactor, and sets the overall project direction. For a workshop, the Sponsor is responsible for: supporting the workshop planning, ensuring that the right participants are in the workshop, providing the project vision at the workshop kick-off and receiving the report out at the end of the workshop. |
| | The **Project Manager** is considered the Workshop Owner and is responsible for: facilitating project planning, execution and closing, establishing workshop goals and desired outcomes, and providing leadership to the project team. |
| | The **Participants** can include: project team, Key Stakeholders, Project Manager and Subject Matter Experts (SME). Steering Committee members and Gatekeepers may also participate in the workshops—although it is more likely that they, like the Sponsor, attend the workshop kick-off and wrap-up sessions. External partners and vendors may also participate in planning workshops. |

| Icon | Role and Primary Responsibility |
|------|--------------------------------|
| | The **Facilitator** is responsible for making it easier for the participants to achieve the workshop goals. The Facilitator works closely with the Project Manager and Sponsor to establish the workshop goals and desired outcomes, then designs the workshop agenda, prepares and runs the workshop. The Facilitator role can be performed by the Project Manager, but it is better to have a neutral party facilitate the workshop so that the Project Manager can be an active participant. |
| | The **Scribe** is responsible for capturing electronically the Project Plan components which are developed and documented on flip charts by the workshop participants. The Scribe works closely with the Facilitator and Project Manager in preparing for the workshop. If there is not a scribe, then the Project Manager should accept the output of the workshop as is: documented on sticky notes and flip chart pages. |

More detail on roles and responsibilities can be found throughout the book.

# Section 2:
# WORKSHOP
# PREPARATION

This section will help you get ready for a workshop with an overview of the Facilitator skills, defining the workshop purpose, creating the agenda, identifying and inviting participants, a list of supplies and finalizing room logistics.

# Skills for the Workshop Facilitator

The Facilitator leads participants through applying the project management techniques to create portions of the Project Charter and achieve the workshop's goals. Easy enough, or is it? A Facilitator needs to:

**Manage the process** – Follow the workshop framework to ensure that

- pre-work has been completed in enough detail to prepare the workshop participants;
- the agenda is developed with the appropriate timing to allow for the open discussion that is needed to reach a common understanding; and
- you are comfortable with the project management techniques and how to modify a technique to be more effective with each unique workshop team.

**Keep the focus** – Work to keep the focus on the topic at hand. The purpose of each project management technique is to provide the focus for the participants. As a Facilitator, you have established the workshop agenda with timing; but remember, timing is an estimate, not an exact science. Some topics may require more time, while other topics may be completed much quicker than planned. Sometimes a conversation that appears to be wandering off is exactly what is needed to allow discovery to occur. So, don't rush the conversation.

When keeping the team focused, the Facilitator, at one extreme, can be a dictator—controlling the timing and the talking. This will lead to a room of participants that will quickly disengage. The other extreme is to facilitate laissez-faire, letting the participants take whatever time they want, meandering off topic as long as they are willing. While this may lead to interesting conversations, it will also lead to disenchanted participants that will wonder if the team will ever reach a conclusion.

So, balance: allow side conversations and flexibility of the agenda as needed. Remind the participants of the purpose of the activity they are working on and ask questions like: "Will this conversation help the team achieve our purpose?" or "Is more or less time needed to achieve our purpose?"

**Act as a resource** – As the Facilitator, your expertise is in the workshop process and application of the project management techniques. While you may be a Subject Matter Expert (SME) on the project topic, it is not your role in this workshop. Let the team make the discovery and the decisions as they develop their Project Plan. Provide information for the team to analyze and determine if they would like to incorporate it into their Project Plan. If the team is asking for support in areas you don't have expertise, find someone who does. You are acting as a resource by connecting the team with the individuals they need to complete their planning.

**Create a positive working environment** – We would all like to be part of an engaging workshop where ideas are shared, discussions occur and decisions are made. Sometimes these conversations can get heated and sometimes one individual may dominate the room. It's your role to ensure that everyone has an equal voice and is treated with respect.

Operating guidelines/ground rules or expectations should be established for the workshop. Establishing operating guidelines empowers the team to self-manage, making the facilitation easier for you. Operating guidelines can include:

- Being fully engaged
- No phones, no computers, and minimize distractions
- Be open to new ideas and different perspectives
- Be willing to listen and work together
- Take ownership of the workshop output

In addition to ground rules, participant expectations can be set using the Think, Feel, Do model. For example:

- Think
  - We have the right knowledge in this room to build an effective plan
  - We can be successful

- Feel
  - There is benefit in collaborating on this effort
  - The work we complete here is necessary for the success of this effort

- Do
  - Engage yourself
  - Be an ambassador and promote the project

# Defining the Workshop Purpose

Each workshop is unique. It is important to start the workshop preparation with the end in mind. What is the purpose of the workshop? What does a successful workshop look like for your project? A workshop could have multiple purposes, for example:

- To provide a specific person or group with a voice in planning
- To provide the entire project team with an opportunity to engage in planning
- To create a high-level plan of an entire project/program
- To create a detailed plan of a portion of the project
- To provide visibility of the complexity of the project to organizational leaders
- To clarify project roles and responsibilities and ensure adequate resource availability
- To gain support for a full-time project manger
- To provide clear connection between the business need and the project approach
- To analyze and de-risk a project

There are many reasons for running a workshop. The Facilitator and Project Manager need to work together to define the purpose and outcome/deliverables for each workshop. When those are defined, then the workshop agenda and participants can be established.

Planning and Closing forms are provided in Appendix A to assist you in preparing for a successful workshop.

# Identifying Workshop Participants

It is critical to get the right people in the room to kick off and plan the project/program. If participants are missing, project components could be omitted and buy-in is incomplete.

A basic approach to identifying workshop participants is to see who within the organization (and sometimes outside of the organization) will be impacted by the project either by working on the project or using the products or services developed by the project.

Representatives or SMEs from each impacted area should be included in some portion of planning. For a smaller project, this could be as few as two or three people; for a larger program, numbers can be much higher. I have run workshops on global programs that had up to fifty participants.

The number of participants will impact how you design and facilitate the workshop and how the room logistics are set up. See **Finalizing Room Logistics** for more details on setting up the room.

Participants can include representation from different organizational functions, such as: Operations, Quality, Marketing, Sales, Legal, Finance, Accounting, Human Resources, Information Technology (Business Analyst, Developers, Testing), and Research and Development.

# Workshop Preparation Roles and Responsibilities

There are clear roles and responsibilities for each individual involved in the workshop. The following is the list of roles and associated responsibilities for workshop preparation (see **Workshop Details** and **Post-Workshop** sections for additional responsibilities):

## Sponsor:
- Meet with the Project Manager and Facilitator to establish expectations for the workshop goal(s) and outcomes
- Prepare to present the project purpose and how the project is prioritized compared to other work in the organization
- Provide support within the organization for participant attendance

## Project Manager:
- Meet with the Sponsor and Facilitator to establish expectations for the workshop goal(s) and outcomes
- Work with the Facilitator to establish the workshop agenda (based on desired goals and outcomes) and how the workshop outcomes will be captured during/post workshop
- Gather existing Project Plans and documentation
- Prepare to present the project history
- Gather input from workshop non-participants to determine how to integrate their thoughts into the workshop discussions and output
- Identify and invite workshop participants
- Identify and send out any pre-read materials to participants
- Set up the workshop location and logistics (travel, accommodations, food, materials and supplies)

## Facilitator:

- Review the **Workshop Details** section of this book to familiarize yourself with the flow of the workshop. The goal of a workshop is to ensure that the project has developed a sufficiently detailed Project Plan (either an entire plan or a portion of a complete plan based on the workshop goal).
- Meet with the Sponsor to:
  - Establish or confirm the purpose and outcomes of the workshop
  - Ask the Sponsor to kick off the workshop by sharing his/her expectations and desired outcomes
  - Ask the Sponsor to return at the end of the workshop so that the participants can report out the progress, next steps and understand the support the team will need for project success
- Meet with the Project Manager to:
  - Establish or confirm the purpose and outcomes of the workshop
  - Review the status of any existing documentation. If planning has already started, then a Project Charter or Business Case could be available. For each document, determine if it:
    - Should be shared with the workshop participants (if yes, determine if the document will be sent out as a pre-read, who will present the document and how much time should be included in the workshop for the presentation)
    - Requires updating before or during the workshop (if yes, determine who needs to participate in the updating of the document)
  - Determine the required participants. Participants may include stakeholders from different functional areas of the organization, such as:  Human Resources, Training, Sales

and Marketing, Finance, Operations/Manufacturing, Purchasing/Supply Chain, Technology/IT, and Regional Facilities, plus external partners (e.g., vendors, contractors and consultants)
  - Determine groupings of participants for completing workshop activities
- Customize the workshop agenda and the supporting PowerPoint file based on the information gathered in the Sponsor and Project Manager meeting
- Meet with those participants that have influence on the project goals or approach to set workshop expectations and clarify workshop roles

## Participants:
- Clear your schedule for the duration of the workshop. A workshop requires active engagement; there will not be time during the workshop to read emails or complete other work
- Review any pre-reads
- Reflect on your thoughts for the project approach, scope, timing and risks

## Scribe:
- Meet with the Project Manager and Facilitator to establish expectations for how the workshop outcomes will be documented
- Gather any templates, forms or software required for documentation

As the Facilitator or Project Manager reading this book, it becomes your responsibility to work with the other individuals and share with them the responsibilities of their role.

# Creating the Workshop Agenda

The duration of a workshop is dependent on the time available, workshop purpose and complexity of the project. A workshop can be as brief as a few hours or as long as a week.

Use the information gathered (purpose, desired outcomes, existing documents and participants) to create your workshop agenda and determine the workshop duration. Use the agenda to update the PowerPoint presentation by adding/updating/removing items in each of the three workshop components:

- Workshop Kick-off – update this section based on the workshop goals, outcomes, agenda, project purpose and history, and how the report out will be shared
- Project Management Techniques – update this section based on the workshop techniques you will be using to develop the workshop outcome
- Wrap-up – update this section based on the specific items that will be reported back to the Sponsor at the end of the session

# Planning Workshop

Every workshop will have a unique agenda. If participants are familiar with project management topics, a simple agenda will do. If the participants have limited exposure to the project management terms, then I often create a more detailed agenda. The following are *simple* agendas for half-day, one-day, three-day and four-day planning workshops. Use these samples along with the information gathered from your meetings with the Project Sponsor and Project Manager to create a custom agenda for your workshop.

Not all of the sample agendas have breaks listed, but all workshops require breaks. A good rule is to schedule a break in the work every 90 minutes. Be flexible, some teams will need shorter breaks more often, while other groups can go longer between breaks. When a group is focused on a topic, they may be happy to continue working longer than the 90 minutes.

## Half Day

This is a simple agenda that can be used for a small project, to focus on a small portion of a larger project or to create a very high-level approach for a larger project. The outcome from a half-day workshop can be valuable, but incomplete. Depending on the size of the project, more time will be needed to develop a detailed Project Plan.

| Estimated Timing | Topic |
|---|---|
| 8:00 – 8:15 | Kick-off |
| 8:15 – 8:45 | Clarify the project goal |
| 8:45 – 10:00 | Deliverables across the time line |
| 10:00 – 10:15 | Break |
| 10:15 – 11:45 | Project Risks |
| 11:45 – 12:00 | Next steps |

## One Day

Workshop start and end times vary for one-day workshops. This workshop agenda challenges the team to start as early as possible and have a working lunch to get the most out of the session. This agenda was used for a project team that had not completed any formal project management training, so a detailed agenda was provided. Note that a full RACI was not applied in this workshop. The workshop only had time to focus on who was accountable and responsible for each deliverable posted on the time line; which we optimistically completed in the scheduled 30 minutes by having each participant write their name (and an A or R) on any deliverable sticky note.

| Estimated Timing | Topic | Details |
|---|---|---|
| 8:30 – 9:00 | Kick-off | Workshop purpose, agenda review, introductions and expectations, confirming the project goal |
| 9:00 – 10:00 | Stakeholder Expectations | Establishing project success criteria by Key Stakeholder |
| 10:00 – 10:15 | Break | |
| 10:15 – 10:30 | Deliverables by Phase | Defining success for each project phase and defining the major activities and final deliverables by phase |
| 10:30 – 11:30 | Time line | Creating the project time line |
| 11:30 – 12:00 | Responsibility by deliverable | Identifying Responsible and Accountable resources for each major activity/deliverable |

| Estimated Timing | Topic | Details |
|---|---|---|
| 12:00 – 12:30 | Lunch | |
| 12:30 – 2:00 | Begin Detailing the Work Breakdown Structure (WBS) | Selecting one deliverable from each functional area, documenting the requirements for each deliverable and the work necessary to create the deliverables in a work package |
| 2:00 – 3:30 | Project Risks | Identifying project risks and determining risk strategies, defining and integrating mitigation strategies into the project time line |
| 3:30 – 4:00 | Close Out | Determine next steps and action items |

## Three Day

This workshop was designed for an international team (hence the use of military time and focus on team building because this team was rarely in one location). The project was actually a large program that had one year of history (explaining the amount of time dedicated to the business justification and project history).

For some organizations and cultures, you never shorten an hour lunch, always allowing for participants to get away from the meeting location during lunch.

| Estimated Timing | DAY 1 | DAY 2 | DAY 3 |
|---|---|---|---|
| 0800 – 1000 | • Welcome <br> • Introductions <br> • Team building | Deliverable identification | • Risk Management Plan <br> • Issue List |
| 1000 – 1200 | Review business justification and project history | Schedule Creation | |
| 1200 – 1300 | Lunch | | |
| 1300 – 1500 | • Lessons Learned <br> • Goal Statement | Schedule Creation (continued) | Communication Plan |
| 1500 – 1700 | Stakeholder Analysis and Success Metrics | Project roles and responsibilities (RACI) | Report Out and Next Steps |

## Four Day

A four-day workshop is a timing luxury that most organizations are not willing to invest in. But, for some projects, based on the level of complexity and the need for detail, a four-day (or sometimes five-day) workshop is the best option. Plus, no one will complain if it is a productive use of their time, and there is a possibility that you finish early.

| Estimated Timing | DAY 1 | DAY 2 | DAY 3 | DAY 4 |
|---|---|---|---|---|
| 9:00 – 10:00 | Kick-off and Business Need | Finalizing Deliverables, Acceptance Criteria and Creating Work Packages | Defining Project Roles | More Risk Management |
| 10:00 – 11:00 | | | | |
| 11:00 – 12:00 | Clarifying the project goal and Gathering Lessons Learned | | | Issue List |
| 12:00 – 1:00 | Lunch | | | |
| 1:00 – 2:00 | Identifying Stakeholders and Analyzing their Key Performance Indicators | Developing the Project Time Line | Identifying, Assessing and Managing Project Risks | Communication Plan |
| 2:00 – 3:00 | | | | |
| 3:00 – 4:00 | Defining Project Deliverables and their Acceptance Criteria | | | Report Out and Next Steps |
| 4:00 – 5:00 | | | | |

# Closing Workshop

While most of this book covers planning components of a project, workshops are a great way to wrap up a project phase or close out a project. However, a closing workshop requires additional preparation by the Project Manager and Facilitator. This preparation can include:

1. Identifying who should be involved in sharing project learnings. Participants of the closing workshop should be as diverse as the participants in the project. Make sure that core and support team members from different organizational areas participate. Each functional group in a project will have different experiences. Their perceptions need to be shared so that an organizational perspective of the project can be formed.

2. Gathering data on the original value promised in a Business Case or Project Charter. There will probably be a large gap when comparing the original value to what is actually delivered. Also, more learning will occur in this comparison than it will when comparing the latest approved baseline to the project actuals.

3. Reviewing the current project baselines for: goal, deliverables, requirements, timing, budget and resources.

4. Gathering and analyzing data on
   a. Project actuals – comparing the actual value delivered to the originally promised value and the current baselines;
   b. Survey of project team – to learn how clearly the team understood the project goals, scope, roles and responsibilities, and the effectiveness of the application of project management and project leadership, as well as lessons learned; and
   c. Survey of stakeholder satisfaction with the project execution and final project outcomes.

5. Determining how lessons learned will be shared with other projects and stakeholders.

6. Defining what happens with un-realized goals/objectives and how outstanding issues or concerns will be handled.

7. Defining how celebrating the project success will be incorporated into the closing workshop.

Sample agenda for closing a major initiative when you are able to invest time in completing the closing preparation:

| Estimated Timing | Topic | Details |
|---|---|---|
| 15 minutes | Opening | Meeting kick-off and introductions (if needed) |
| 15 minutes | Project Summary | Goals achieved, value delivered, comparisons of actuals to original value defined in the Project Charter or Business Case, and current baselines |
| 20 minutes | Stakeholder Satisfaction | Stakeholder survey findings (this could be presented by the Sponsor) |
| 20 minutes | Team Survey | Team member survey findings on project clarity, project management application, leadership and lessons learned |
| 20 – 40 minutes | Lessons Learned | Apply the Gathering Lessons Learned workshop technique and apply Alternative three (see page 61) |

| Estimated Timing | Topic | Details |
|---|---|---|
| 10 minutes | Next Steps | Defining how the information gathered in this session will be shared within the organization |
|  | Celebration | Celebrate the progress made by the team |

Sample agenda for a quick gathering of participants' input on lessons learned:

| Estimated Timing | Topic | Details |
|---|---|---|
| 10 minutes | Opening | Project summary, meeting purpose and introductions (if needed) |
| 20 – 40 minutes | Lessons Learned | Apply the Gathering Lessons Learned workshop technique and apply Alternative three (see page 61) |
| 5 minutes | Meeting Close Out and Next Steps | Defining how the information gathered in this session will be shared within the organization |

# Inviting Participants

Once the workshop purpose is defined and participants are identified, it is time send invitations. If the agenda is not yet developed, and the workshop does not occur for some time, you might send a save-the-date notification so that the event can be added to the participants' calendars. Here is a simple calendar notification or email:

*Save the Date. Your participation is required/requested in a planning workshop for Project _____ (project name) on xx/xx/xxxx. Details to follow.*

A formal invitation should be sent for all workshops. A well-written invitation serves multiple purposes; it:

- Notifies participants of the event
- Shares logistic information
- Provides an opportunity for management to show their support
- Communicates project alignment within organizational priorities
- Shows that the event is well planned (by sharing the purpose, participants and agenda)

Here is a draft of an invitation. Feel free to modify it and use it for your workshops.

*Subject: Project _____ (project name) Planning Workshop*

*A Project Plan is being created for the _____ (project name) project. In order to create a comprehensive Project Plan, your presence is required/requested. This project has full support of management.*

*The purpose of the workshop is _____.*

*Other individuals participating in the workshop include: _____ (this can include a list of names or names and functional areas represented)*

*The workshop will be held at _____ (workshop location, if the workshop is off-site, include the location address, parking or any other related logistics).*

*The agenda is (I rarely put timing on the agenda shared in an invitation except the start and end times):*

| *Topic* | *Details* |
|---|---|
| *8:00 am Kick-off* | *Workshop purpose, agenda review, introductions and expectations, confirming the project goal* |
| *Stakeholder Expectations* | *Establishing project success criteria by key stakeholder* |
| *Deliverables by Phase* | *Defining success for each project phase and defining the major activities and final deliverables by phase* |
| *Time Line* | *Creating the project time line* |

| *Topic* | *Details* |
|---------|-----------|
| *Responsibility by Deliverable* | *Identifying Responsible and Accountable resources for each major activity/deliverable* |
| *Lunch* | |
| *Begin Detailing the WBS* | *Selecting one deliverable from each functional area and documenting the requirements for each deliverable as well as the work necessary to create the deliverable* |
| *Project Risks* | *Identifying project risks and determining risk strategies, defining and integrating mitigation strategies into the project time line* |
| *Close Out 4:30pm* | *Determine next steps and action items* |

*The workshop will be a working session. Plan to be engaged for the entire session. The workshop starts promptly at _____ (time) and runs until _____(time). Let the Project Manager know if you need assistance in rescheduling other events.*

*I look forward to your active participation in planning this project,*

*Senior Manager, VP (Signature of Project Sponsor)*

It can be more effective to have the Sponsor or other high-level management send out the invitation. The Facilitator or the Project Manager will probably have to draft the invitation for the Sponsor to review, modify and send.

A quick reference for participant invitations is located in Appendix B.

# Workshop Supplies

Many trainers and facilitators have a *tool kit* filled with common supplies. If you will be running frequent workshops, build your own tool kit. This will save you from running around at the last minute, trying to secure supplies. Your supply list will depend on the workshop techniques selected. In general, you will need:

## Tool Kit Supplies
- Sticky notes (recommended in various colors and sizes—different colors may be used to represent items by functional area, project phases or programs within a project)
- Flip charts and brown paper roll (for the time line)
- Fat colored magic markers to write on the flip chart pages
- Fine colored magic markers to write on the sticky notes
- Masking tape or painters tape
- Scissors
- Participant name tents or tags (if participants don't know each other well)

## Additional items
- PowerPoint presentation of slides used to facilitate the workshop
- Templates or other handouts—some workshop participants like handouts of the slides

# Finalizing Room Logistics

Getting the logistics right will help the participants focus on the activities of the workshop. When thinking through logistics, consider a room set-up that allows for:

- Movement of the participants and the facilitator
- Comfortable configuration of the space that promotes conversation and increases the opportunity for eye contact
- Space for flip charts, computer, projection screen and facilitator supplies
- Wall space for documenting activities
- Minimizing disruptions from daily operations

Table set-up can be an important factor in establishing the right collaborative environment. If there are eight or less participants, working at a conference table can work effectively. For eight to twelve participants, a U-shape or semi-circle provide good options. Any more than twelve, breaking the group into smaller table teams of three to four is effective (I find that teams of five often have two or three participants working and the other participants having side conversations). Table teams can be established randomly or you can intentionally create diverse table teams by splitting the teams up by project roles or functional areas. Here is a sample room layout:

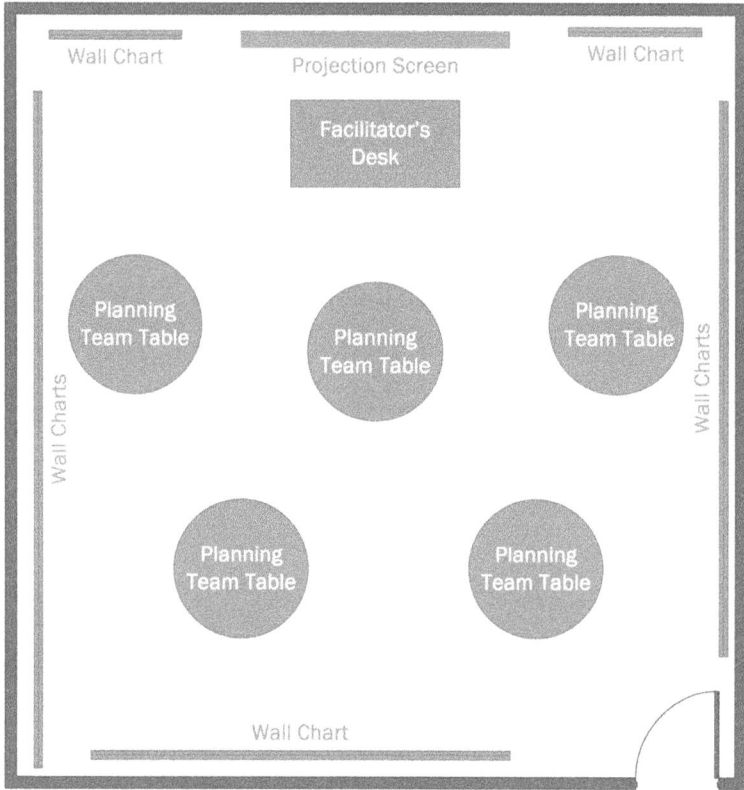

Room set-up is often constrained by what is available. Avoid rooms that have a classroom feel (rows of tables where everyone faces the front). Be creative with what you have and be willing to show up early in case you need to move furniture around to create better space for the team.

# Section 3:
# WORKSHOP DETAILS

This section contains detailed instructions for preparing and facilitating each workshop component.

# Workshop Details Overview

This section of the book provides details for each of the project management techniques, including:

- Purpose – of the technique
- Outcome – what is created at the end of applying the technique
- Technique Review – basic overview of the project management technique
- Supplies – any specific materials used in applying the technique
- Potential Slides and Sample Output– to use in setting up and explaining the use of the technique in a workshop activity as well as photographs of what the outcome of the technique might look like (see Appendixes C and D for a quick reference to all slides and output used throughout this book)
- Timing – the range of time it can take to apply the technique
- Directions – step-by-step instructions for using the technique
- Alternatives – flexible approaches to applying the technique when you want to modify the directions
- Recommended Debriefs – ideas for providing closure after applying the technique
- Integration – questions to ask the participants to ensure that all parts of the Project Plan work together to achieve the project goal

It is assumed that the Facilitator is leading each part of the workshop unless it is clearly stated that the Sponsor or Project Manager is leading.

Here is a quick overview of the three main parts of a workshop:

## Kick-off

- Welcome – establishes the workshop purpose and expectations
- Sponsor Kick-off – provides the business justification for the project
- Project Manager Kick-off – shares workshop expectations and project history

**Project Management Techniques** – Specific techniques can be applied based on the workshop's need. These techniques include:

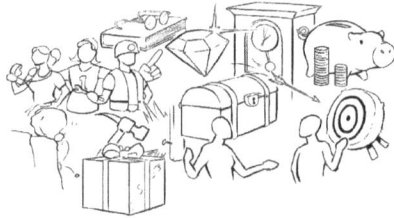

- Clarifying the project goal
- Gathering lessons learned
- Analyzing Stakeholders and their Key Performance Indicators (KPI)
- Brainstorming project deliverables
- Defining deliverable acceptance criteria
- Developing the project time line
- Defining project roles and responsibilities
- Identifying, assessing and managing project risks
- Documenting project issues
- Creating the communication plan
- Project Closing

## Wrap-Up

The Report Out is presented to the Project Sponsor (and additional leadership representation, such as the Steering Committee and Gatekeepers).

Close Out of the workshop is completed and next steps are determined.

# Workshop Roles and Responsibilities

Each individual involved has a role and specific responsibilities during the workshop.

| Role | Responsibilities in Workshop |
|---|---|
| **Sponsor** | • Kick-off workshop by providing business justification for project work<br>• Attend workshop wrap-up, asking questions and providing feedback on the information presented |
| **Project Manager** | • Present the project history<br>• Provide the example for active engagement in the workshop activities: effective listening and open communication<br>• Be an active workshop participant or, if your presence in the workshop minimizes candid conversation, be prepared to excuse yourself and identify a specific time with the facilitator you can step back in to answer questions or review progress<br>• Lead the wrap-up and definition of next steps |
| **Facilitator** | • Facilitate the workshop<br>• Work with the Scribe to ensure that he/she is capturing the correct information in the correct format<br>• Work with the Project Manager to adjust the timing or topics based on the pace and discussions occurring during the workshop<br>• Adjust the timing of the agenda to accommodate the actual time it takes to complete project management techniques. (Some techniques may need to be covered quickly in order to spend more time on higher priority items.) |

| Role | Responsibilities in Workshop |
|---|---|
| **Participants** | • Actively participate<br>• Listen with an open mind to others' ideas<br>• Adhere to the workshop expectations |
| **Scribe** | • Support Facilitator during the workshop<br>• Begin creating electronic versions of the completed workshop techniques |

# Kick-Off

## Workshop Welcome

### Purpose
Welcome participants to the workshop, set the expectations for the session, and share enthusiasm for the workshop and the expectation that everyone should be actively engaged

### Outcome
Expectations set for fully engaged participants

### Technique Review
There are no project management techniques used in the Workshop Welcome.

### Supplies
Slides for reviewing each of the workshop components—purpose, outcome, agenda, introductions, expectations and report out

### Potential Slides

**Collaborative Workshop**
WELCOME

Agenda

| Estimated Timing | Topics |
| --- | --- |
| 8:00 – 9:30 | Sponsor Kick-off, Introductions, Ground Rules & Expectations |
| 9:30 – 9:45 | Break |
| 9:45 – 10:15 | Lessons Learned |
| 10:15 – 11:00 | Stakeholders |
| 11:00 – 12:00 | Deliverables & Time Line |
| 12:00 – 1:00 | Lunch |
| 1:00 – 2:30 | Risk & Issues |
| 2:30 – 2:45 | Break |
| 2:45 – 3:00 | RACI |
| 3:00 – 3:30 | Communications |
| 3:30 – 4:00 | Financials |
| 4:00 – 4:15 | Report out Preparation |
| 4:15 – 5:00 | Report out to Sponsor |

### Purpose

- Purpose: Develop a project plan to achieve the project goal
- Output:
  - Working Project Plan for the project including: stakeholder assessment, goals, deliverables, time line, risks, issues, responsibilities, communication plan and estimated financials
  - Report out to our Sponsor
- Excluding: list any items, that need to be identified, that will not be included in the workshop

### Beginning with the End in Mind

- What we will report out to the Sponsor at the end of the workshop:

| Topic | What we Accomplished | Next Steps | Support Needed |
|---|---|---|---|
| Stakeholder assessment | | | |
| Scope: goals & deliverables | | | |
| Time / Schedule | | | |
| Risks & Issues | | | |
| Costs / Financials | | | |
| Human Resources / RACI | | | |
| Communications | | | |

### Ground Rules

- Be fully engaged
- No phones
- No computers
- Be open to new ideas and different perspectives
- Take ownership of the workshop output

### Introductions

- Name
- Role
- How you can contribute to the success of this project

## Timing

30 – 60 minutes

## Directions

1. Welcome participants to the workshop and review the workshop:
   - **Purpose** – Share the purpose of the workshop; for example, in this workshop, we will work together to plan how the project goal will be achieved
   - **Outcomes** – Review what will be created in the workshop; for example, deliverables, time lines, risk log . . .
   - **Agenda** – Review the major topics and timing; indicate that there is a lot of work to be done and that all participants are responsible for the workshop's success. The agenda may fluctuate, activities may take more or less time than scheduled
   - **Expectations/Ground Rules** – Review the agreed upon behavior during the workshop (for example: willing to reach

consensus, being fully engaged, no phones, no computers, listening with an open mind to others' ideas, and taking ownership of the materials created and the decisions made)

- **Report Out** – The session will end with a report out to leadership on the project strategy and the decision(s) made for the project. Review the format that will be used to communicate the workshop progress: topics covered, what was accomplished, next steps and support needed from the Project Sponsor

2. Have all participants introduce themselves and how they will contribute to the success of this project.

## Alternatives

1. The Kick-off is best led by the Facilitator, but it can be shared between the Facilitator and the Project Manager.

2. During introductions (or even when returning from breaks) can be a good time to integrate team building activities into the workshop. If you select a team building activity, make sure that it is purposeful for the participants and the project. The Facilitator and Project Manager should work together to find appropriate team building activities. Activities I use include:

   a. Using an instrument like DiSC° or Myer-Briggs to help team members understand themselves and how they interact with others
   b. Completing an activity like the marshmallow tower challenge (https://www.ted.com/talks/tom_wujec_build_a_tower) to help teams understand the value of testing out uncertainty early in the project

3. Have the participants establish their own ground rules for the workshop.

Utilize the Think, Feel, Do strategy to welcome participants and set up the workshop purpose and guide the creation of the plan. For example:

### Think
- This workshop is a good thing for you, the project and the organization
- This workshop will help develop a common strategy for achieving the project goal

### Feel
- Proud of the deliverables created in the workshop
- A collaborative planning process will end with a better, faster, more accurate plan

### Do
- Engage yourself during the workshop
- Embrace the process; be an ambassador to collaborative planning during and after the workshop
- Hold each other accountable

## Recommended Debrief
After the Workshop Welcome is completed, ask if there are any questions about the workshop flow or expectations before we move to the Sponsor kick-off.

## Integration
There is no integration needed for this portion of the workshop.

# Sponsor Kick-off

### Purpose
Have the Sponsor provide the business justification for the project, what the project should achieve and why it is important to the organization

### Outcome
Fully informed participants and clearly defined project priority

### Technique Review
There are no project management techniques used in the Sponsor Kick-off.

### Supplies
Existing documentation for the project (e.g., Project Charter, Business Case, Marketing Strategy). Slides may be created for sharing this information, or this information could be sent out to participants as a pre-read.

### Potential Slide

Kick-off
_____

• A word from our Sponsor:
  • Project Background
    • *Na oiaoiif s ijreroirodl  jpd a'*
    • *A ajfaid*
    • *Asl iijf gjitti ad' jma't riij mtjuptg gs gri gj oti s gyupet*

### Timing
15 – 60 minutes

## Directions

Have the Sponsor share:

1. The importance of this workshop, of being fully engaged during the workshop and their expectations for the workshop outcome.

2. What the Sponsor's attendance at the workshop will be; for example, they will be back for a report out on the progress made at the end of the workshop.

3. The purpose of the project and the business need or value driving the project, as well as reviewing business documentation that may have been created.

4. How this project is aligned with the organization's strategy and the priority of this project versus other work within the organization.

## Alternatives

1. There are limited alternatives to having the Sponsor kick-off the workshop and share the business need for the project. If the Sponsor is not available, then an alternative leader in the organization may be selected (e.g., Project Manager, Key Stakeholder, Steering Committee member or Gatekeeper) to present the information. The information must be presented to create a common vision and fully inform workshop participants. The Sponsor can Skype in or record a personal video to share at the kick-off.

2. The Sponsor Kick-off is a great time for the team to speak up and ask for clarity of purpose (be careful that the questions don't turn into a tactical conversation of the project approach)—the questions should focus on understanding the business need and any business constraints on the project.

3. When the Sponsor kicks off the workshop, you should be ready for anything. Even though the agenda has the Sponsor kick-off prior to introductions, the Sponsor might stop talking, look around and say, "I don't know everyone here, can you introduce yourself and what department you represent?" Be flexible and let the introductions occur early. If you had planned on participants sharing something about the project, that portion of the introductions can be completed later in the session.

### Recommended Debrief
After the Sponsor Kick-off is completed, thank the Sponsor for their time and ask if there are any quick questions for the Sponsor about the specific project before the workshop moves to the next section.

### Integration
There is no integration needed for this portion of the workshop.

# Project Manager Kick-off

## Purpose
To welcome participants, share their enthusiasm for the workshop and the expectation that everyone should be actively engaged, as well as updating the participants of any work that has already occurred on the project or in project planning

## Outcome
Environment of trust

## Technique Review
There are no project management techniques used in the Project Manager Kick-off.

## Supplies
Slides that support sharing the Project Manager's Kick-off and project history

## Potential Slide

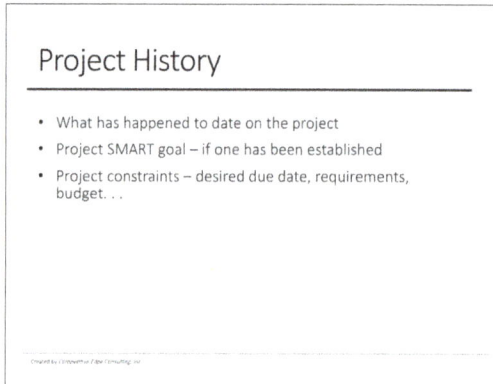

## Timing
15 – 30 minutes

## Directions

Have the Project Manager share the project history. If the project has already started, have the Sponsor, Project Manager or lead team member share the existing project strategy and the work completed to date.

## Alternatives

1.  If the Project Manager is not available, the Facilitator can share this information.

2.  If there is no history, there may still be implied expectations that should be shared with the team.

## Recommended Debrief

After the Project Manager Kick-off is completed, thank the Project Manager for the information they shared and their support of the workshop. Ask if there are any quick questions for the Project Manager about the history of the project before the workshop moves to the next section.

## Integration

There is no integration needed for this portion of the workshop.

# Project Management Techniques

## Clarifying the Project Goal

### Purpose
To create a common vision for what the project will achieve

### Outcome
Goal statement

### Technique Review
The goal is a component of the project scope. Scope is defined as: the project goal, project deliverables, requirements (also referred to as acceptance criteria or quality) and the work necessary to create each deliverable at the level of quality defined in the requirements.

A common acronym used to establish a project goal is SMART. If you search the Internet, you will find various definitions of the SMART acronym. Use the definition that is the best fit for your organization. I use the definition described here:

S    **S**pecific – defines a common and clear project focus. Because we all bring different ideas and perspectives to the project, having a specific goal removes ambiguity.

*M* Measurable – defines how project success will be measured. The measure of success can be quantitative or qualitative. It should align with the project success criteria of your Stakeholders.

*A* Action – The action portion of the goal statement is a verb that sets the overall project direction, but not the project approach. There are numerous potential approaches to achieve a project goal. The project approach may change, but the overall project direction is less likely to change.

*R* Realistic – determines if the SMART goal can be achieved. This is a simple but quick gut check, based on your past experience.

*T* Time-bound – defines when the project goal will be achieved. A caution about time-bound: do not create arbitrary due dates. If mandatory forces require a specific end date, then use that date. If there is not a mandated date, then let the work and the resources available determine the time frame of the project.

## Supplies

Slides to facilitate the technique and flip charts with markers for each table team and for the facilitator

## Potential Slides

| Defining the Goal | Revisiting the Goal |
|---|---|
| • Now that we have a common understanding of the project's purpose, let's clarify the project goal using the SMART criteria: <br>  • Specific <br>  • Measurable <br>  • Actionable <br>  • Realistic <br>  • Time-bound <br> • In teams, and in your own words, define the goal of the project in a single simple sentence <br> • Document your goal statement on the flip chart | • Now that we have a common vision of the project, let's confirm the project goal <br> • In teams, and in your own words, define the goal of the project in a single simple sentence <br> • Document your goal statement on the flip chart |

## Timing
15 – 60 minutes

## Directions
1. Review the importance of working as a team toward a common goal. If a common goal is not created, each team member will determine the project purpose and success criteria themselves. Having a stated goal that meets the SMART criteria helps the team remain focused on a common definition of success.

2. Review the SMART criteria.

3. Have each workshop participant, individually, document a SMART goal statement after being given the project purpose presented by the Sponsor.

4. Once each individual has documented a goal, take turns having them each read their goal statement. Using components of each statement, facilitate the creation of one goal statement. This can take some time and patience, but it is worth the effort. If there are different opinions of the project goal, then it will be impossible to agree on an overall project approach.

5. Write the goal statement on a flip chart and hang it on the wall for reference throughout the workshop.

## Alternatives
1. Skip this if the goal statement was just presented in the kick-off.

2. Depending on the number of participants, you might want to modify the directions:
   a. For up to six people, complete the directions as provided above.
   b. For more than six participants, break them up into small groups (three to five participants per team), and have each

group create a goal statement and document it on team flip charts. Have each team report out their goal statement for the project and use the small group goal statements to create one project goal statement.

3.  After the team has spent time planning the project, they may have an updated, clearer, well-articulated and internalized SMART goal. Always revisit the goal statement at the end of the workshop. Ask the team members to restate the project goal in their own words—and work together to create a singular goal statement.

## Recommended Debrief

After you have facilitated defining the project goal statement, ask, "Does the goal statement clearly define:
  - What the project will achieve?
  - What success looks like?
  - How we will know when the project is done?"

## Integration

Throughout the workshop, refer back to the goal statement to ensure that the components of the Project Plan is focused on achieving the project goal.

# Gathering Lessons Learned from Previous Projects

*BEST PRACTICES* | *EVENTS TO AVOID*

## Purpose
To share learning from other project experiences and this project in order to determine what should be repeated and avoided for the benefit of this project. This activity gets everyone actively involved and provides an opportunity to model that everyone has experiences that bring value to the workshop.

## Outcome
List of Best Practices and Events to Avoid

## Technique Review
Leveraging past learning formally gathers what is already known that will help drive project success. There are two approaches for leveraging past learning—individual conversations and team brainstorming—and both can provide great value to planning. Here, we will focus on team brainstorming.

## Supplies
Slides to facilitate the technique, sticky pads and markers for each table, and two flip chart pages

## Potential Slide and Sample Output

## Timing
20 – 40 minutes

## Directions
1. Title two flip chart pages:
   - Best Practices – these are activities that provide value to the project's efficiency and effectiveness that should be continued as the project continues (positives)
   - Events to Avoid – these are activities that would provide challenges to the project and are best to be avoided (negatives)

2. Review the value of bringing past experience to planning this project.

3. Ask the workshop participants to discuss, at their tables, their experiences on this or past projects and identify items for each flip chart page. Have them write as many positive items (Best Practices) and challenges (Events to Avoid) as they can on sticky notes. Only one item per sticky. Give the tables 15 minutes to finish this.

4. Have each table/team place their sticky notes on the appropriate flip chart page.

## Alternatives

1.  If time is limited, this activity can be modified or skipped. As a modification, review the value of bringing past experiences to planning and, when identifying project deliverables later in the workshop, ask participants to include best practices in their deliverables (e.g., standing meetings or setting up a project SharePoint site).

2.  If this technique is used during a project that is currently in execution, just change the flip chart headers from *Events to Avoid* to *Events to Avoid or Stop*.

3.  If this technique is used during a phase or project closing workshop, you might want to make two changes:
    a.  The questions asked can be modified to "If we had to do this project again, what should we repeat?" and "What activities should be avoided?" Or "What should other projects learn from us to repeat and to avoid?"
    b.  The flip chart headers can be labeled *Lessons Learned for Other Projects* and *Events for Other Projects to Avoid.*

## Recommended Debrief

After you have facilitated the creation on lessons learned and they are posted to the flip chart pages:

*   Have a volunteer read each of the sticky notes on the positive flip chart. Congratulate them for what they have been doing well. Challenge them to continue doing these items and ensure that they are integrated into this project.

*   Have a volunteer read each of the sticky notes on the challenges flip chart. If an item is an Issue or a Risk, place a star on it as an indication that these items will be addressed later in the workshop. Challenge each workshop participant to

take appropriate action to remove these challenges from the plan that is being developed in this workshop.

## Integration

Throughout the workshop, refer back to the two flip charts and ask, "Based on your Best Practices and Events to Avoid, is there anything that should be added or removed from the Project Plan?"

# Analyzing Stakeholders and Their Key Performance Indicators (KPI)

## Purpose
Identify Key Stakeholders and what project success looks like for each stakeholder

## Outcome
Identified and prioritized stakeholders defined success metrics. Optional outcome: level of stakeholder engagement and strategies for engaging each stakeholder. (The terms KPI, success metrics and success criteria are often used interchangeably.)

## Technique Review
A stakeholder is anyone who is actively involved in the project, or impacted by the execution or completion of the project. Stakeholders have expectations of what the project will deliver. A stakeholder can be anyone; for example, a stakeholder can be a customer, client, vendor, partner, government, regulatory body, user, peer, team member or organizational leadership. Stakeholders have the ability to influence a project—they can be supportive or create obstacles that could delay or stop the project.

There are three steps to the discipline of stakeholder management:

1. Stakeholder identification and prioritization
2. Stakeholder success criteria or Key Performance Indicators (KPI) identification
3. Stakeholder engagement and strategy development

For the workshop, you can select which step provides the most value. If time permits, complete all three steps.

## Supplies

Slides to facilitate the technique, sticky notes and markers for each participant, and two flip chart pages

## Potential Slide and Sample Output

### Defining Stakeholders

- Purpose: To identify key stakeholders and what is critical to success from their perspective

- Directions:
    1. Identify key stakeholders, write each stakeholder on a sticky note
    2. Place the stakeholder on the Prioritization Chart
    3. For your assigned stakeholders:
        - *Discuss what their interests and concerns may be*
        - *Define their success metrics*

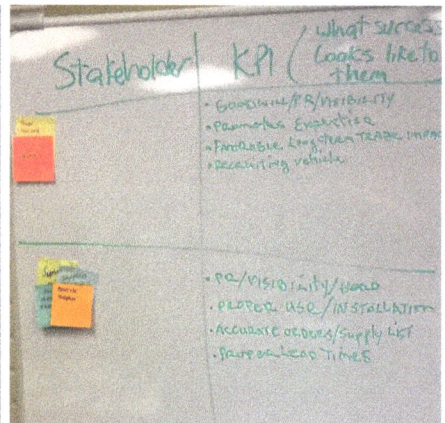

## Timing

30 – 60 minutes

## Directions

*Step One*

1. You will need two flip chart pages. One with a 2x2 matrix for stakeholder interest and power, and another with two columns labeled *Stakeholder* and *KPI*—label additional columns if you are completing level of engagement.

*Step Two*

2. Review the definition of a stakeholder. State that each stakeholder will be prioritized, but first they need to be identified.

3. Ask the participants to identify all the stakeholders they can for the project, writing one stakeholder per sticky note.

4. Review the 2x2 stakeholder prioritization matrix. Have each participant determine the level of power and (desired) interest of their stakeholder and place the sticky note accordingly on the 2x2 matrix. Give them a few minutes to complete this step. If there are duplicate stakeholders on sticky notes, those sticky notes can just be stacked on top of each other on the 2x2 matrix.

5. Once all the prioritization is completed, have each participant report the rationale behind where they posted each stakeholder. Ensure that all workshop participants agree to the stakeholder placement on the matrix.

*Step Three*

6. Gather all the stakeholders in the high-power and high-interest cell. Split them equally between the table teams (for more information on establishing table teams refer to **Finalizing Room Logistics**).

7. Ask the table teams to identify and document on their flip charts the three to four top project KPI per stakeholder—what

the stakeholder is most interested in as an outcome of the project. Give the teams a few minutes to complete this step.

*Step Four*

8.  Ask the table teams to identify the current level of engagement of each assigned stakeholder and the level of engagement that is desirable for the project to be successful. If your organization follows a behavioral (or organizational) change management process that your workshop participants are familiar with, use that. I use the following definitions:

| Level of Engagement | Description |
|---|---|
| Unaware | No idea that the project exists |
| Aware | Aware of the project, but not aware of any project details |
| Understand | Aware of the project, and understands the project purpose, project strategy and key details of the project |
| Collaborate | Willing to work together with the project team as requested to support the project |
| Commit | Willing to dedicate time and/or resources to complete project work |
| Advocate | Proactively supports the project through actions and communications |

9.  If there is a gap between the current and the desired level, have the team identify a strategy to gain the appropriate level of stakeholder engagement.
10. Have each team report out their work and ensure agreement from all workshop participants.

## Alternatives

1.  There is rarely enough time to complete all three steps in the stakeholder management technique. If there is enough time, complete steps one and two (stakeholder identification, prioritizing and KPI). A simple alternative is to ask the group to identify who they believe are the top three or four stakeholders and identify the KPI for each of them.

2.  If there is enough time and the project warrants the additional effort, then KPI can be identified for the stakeholders ranked as high interest and low power.

## Recommended Debrief

After facilitating the stakeholder technique, remind participants

*   About the value of defining project success from the perspective of each Key Stakeholder and
*   The success criteria should be revisited throughout the workshop, ensuring that the project approach delivers to Key Stakeholder success criteria.

## Integration

All components of the Project Plan must work together to achieve to the project goal. To ensure this, ask if the KPIs support the project goal.

Throughout the workshop, refer back to the stakeholder's KPI to ensure that the work being planned will meet the KPIs.

# Defining Project Deliverables

## Purpose

Provide clarity to the project scope by defining major project activities and deliverables

## Outcome

List of project deliverables

## Technique Review

Deliverables are components of the project scope. Scope is defined as the project goal, project deliverables, requirements (also referred to as acceptance criteria or quality) and the work necessary to create each deliverable at the level of quality defined in the requirements.

Once the project goal is defined, identifying what your project will deliver is the heart of project scoping. There are three categories of deliverables on all projects: final, interim and project management. Here is a definition of each deliverable category along with a small sample of potential deliverables.

**Final deliverables** are those deliverables turned over at the end of the project to meet the business need. Final deliverables can include, but are not limited to:

Facilities, projects, policies, metrics, software, documentation, procedures, training, training curriculum, annual meetings, consumer products and services . . .

The list of potential project deliverables is as long as, or longer than, the list of potential projects. So, it is critical that you gain agreement with the Sponsor and Key Stakeholders on the final deliverables for your project.

**Interim deliverables** are those deliverables that need to be developed before the end of the project to support the creation of the final deliverables. Interim deliverables can include, but are not limited to:

Designs, layouts, documentation, training strategies, implementation plans, test plans, organizational change management plans, maintenance plans, requirements, designs, drafts, pilots, prototypes, samples, benchmarking . . .

As you review the list, you may think some items listed here could be used as final deliverables, and you are right. Depending on the project, what serves as an interim deliverable on one project, may be a final deliverable on another project.

It is also possible, on small projects, that there are no interim deliverables, only final and project management deliverables.

**Project Management deliverables** are the most under-scoped category of deliverables. They are created to manage the project, motivate the team and provide project communications. Project management deliverables include:

Communications, meeting agendas and meeting minutes, budgets, contracts, status reports, project metrics, rewards and recognition, Project Plan updates, Project Evaluation, and Lessons Learned.

Even when these deliverables are not included in the project planning, you will still be responsible for creating them. However, you will not have scheduled the time, resources and cost to create them.

## Supplies

Slides to facilitate the technique and sticky notes for each participant or table team

## Potential Slide and Sample Output

## Timing

30 – 60 minutes

## Directions

Have participants identify the specific deliverables that will need to be created for the project by answering each of the following questions and documenting each deliverable on an individual sticky note.

- What needs to be turned over at the end of the project to meet the business need?
- What needs to be developed before the end of the project to support the creation of the final deliverables and drive the change required by the project?
- What needs to be created to meet Stakeholder KPI?
- What needs to be created to manage the project, motivate the team and provide project communications?

## Alternatives

1. Each workshop participant can focus on identifying only the deliverables that they will be responsible for (if using this approach, it is important that all project areas participate in the workshop).

2. Color code the deliverables by having specific roles or departments use assigned colors of markers or sticky notes. This will create a visual understanding of where project work is being completed.

## Recommended Debrief

After facilitating the deliverable identification, determine if the list of deliverables should be reviewed at this time, or, if the workshop is applying the Acceptance Criteria technique or developing the project time line, the deliverables will be reviewed then. If no other technique will be used at this time, the deliverable sticky notes can be saved for future project planning and documentation.

## Integration

In order to ensure that what has already been planned is consistent with the work just completed, ask:

- If these deliverables are created, will the project achieve the project goal?
- Will the project satisfy the stakeholders' KPI?
- Do any deliverables have to be added or deleted to integrate lessons learned?

# Defining Project Deliverables Acceptance Criteria/ Requirements

## Purpose
Provide clarity to what each project deliverable will contain

## Outcome
List of prioritized acceptance criteria by project deliverables

## Technique Review
Acceptance Criteria (sometimes referred to as Requirements) is a component of the project scope. Acceptance Criteria or Requirements define the expectations of a project or deliverable. For example, the requirements for a training deliverable might include:

- Must be completed in less than one business day
- Must contain hands-on experience using case studies
- Must include online job aids post training
- Should have participants selected by management
- Could have electronic copies of the materials

Make sure that each requirement provides measurable or quantifiable expectations of what the deliverable will contain or be able to do. Requirements such as "better, faster, friendlier" provide more ambiguity than clarity. Each requirement will be prioritized using *must haves, should haves, and could haves.*

## Supplies

Slides to facilitate the technique, flip chart paper and the list or sticky notes of deliverables from the previous technique

## Potential Slide and Sample Output

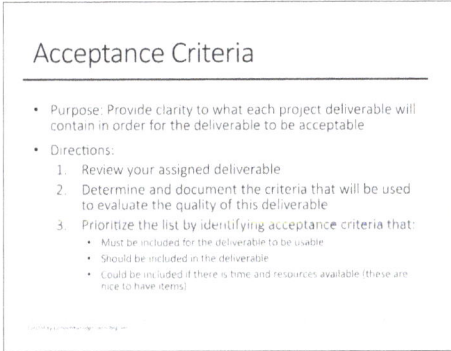

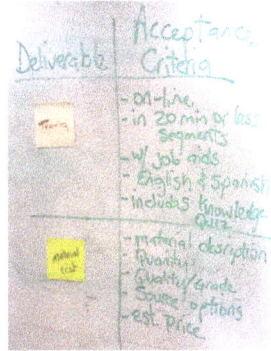

## Timing

30 – 60 minutes

## Directions

1.  Assign one deliverable to a team.

2.  Have each team discuss the deliverable and flip chart the acceptance criteria.

3.  Once the acceptance criteria list for a deliverable is completed, have the team prioritize the list by identifying acceptance criteria that:
    a.  Must be included for the deliverable to be usable
    b.  Should be included in the deliverable
    c.  Could be included if there is time and resources available (these are nice-to-have items)

4.  Have each team report out their deliverable acceptance criteria and make sure that the team agrees with the commitment.

## Alternatives

Skip this technique completely in the workshop; this work can be completed outside of the workshop by the individual accountable for the deliverable.

Select only key deliverables for the group to work on during the workshop.

## Recommended Debrief

After facilitating the creation of deliverable acceptance criteria, reinforce how this technique will:

- Reduce assumptions about what each deliverable is and what a deliverable is not
- Increase the accuracy of estimating the resources and effort required to build each deliverable

## Integration

You must ensure that what has already been planned is consistent with the work completed. To do that, ask:

- Does the clarity of these deliverables alter anything we have already discussed in the workshop?
- Do the acceptance criteria support the stakeholder KPIs and project goal?

# Developing the Project Time Line

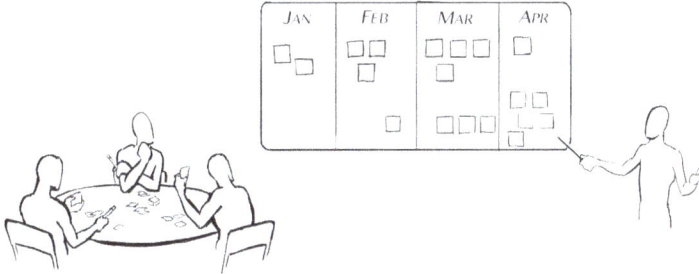

## Purpose
Collaboratively build the project time line

## Outcome
Project schedule at the deliverable/major activity level

## Technique Review
The schedule is the visual representation of the project work over time. For the workshop, focus on the major activities/deliverables in the project.

Deliverables that are created in the near term tend to be more detailed and clearly defined; deliverables created later in the project may be vague. For example, there may be clarity in the work needed to design an item; but, if the design is not complete, all the components needed to create the design have limited clarity. This is a prime example of why planning is ongoing.

There are two general approaches to creating a schedule:

- Listing out all the deliverables across a time line based on the sequence in which each deliverable will be created. This will establish when the project is scheduled to be complete. In this approach, the value of the project is not achieved until all the deliverables are created and the project is completed—this is often referred to as a traditional or waterfall approach.

- Defining short durations of time (two to six weeks) in which a deliverable that is valuable to the end user of the project will be completed. This short duration of time is called *iteration*. A project using this approach can have many iterations. Once all the iterations are completed, the entire value of the project is achieved. At the end of any iteration, a decision can be made to reprioritize work or stop the project. This approach is referred to as an iterative or agile approach.

Determine which approach is a best fit for the project and your organization, and step up the time line creation accordingly.

## Supplies
Slides to facilitate the technique, major activities/deliverable sticky notes from the Defining Project Deliverables technique, brown paper roll and tape

## Potential Slide and Sample Output

## Timing
60 - 120 minutes

## Directions

Set-up – Tape brown paper to the wall. Make sure the paper is long enough to build the schedule for your project. Begin with today and determine the cadence—is it: weeks, months, quarters or years? If the project is following a stage-gate or lifecycle process, make sure you label the time line with the stages or phases of the process that is being followed. Instead of labeling the brown paper with timing, write the timing on a sticky note and place it above the brown paper. In the photo, green sticky notes turned on the diagonal (like dimonds) are used to show the progress of time. (I prefer this in place of writing dates on the brown paper because, as the schedule develops, dates may get moved around.)

1. Review any existing schedule or time line expectations if there are any.

2. Individually:
   a. Review deliverables and major activities for the project from the previous technique.
   b. Have participants place their sticky notes on the time line under the timing that the activity will occur (either when work begins on the deliverable or when the deliverable will be completed).

3. Once all the sticky notes are posted, have the entire group stand around the time line while each participant presents the activities and deliverables they posted on the time line. (If individuals cannot stand for a long period of time, they should be welcome to sit. I find that having people stand keeps them focused on the workshop topic and not other topics.) Encourage conversation so that missing activities/deliverables are discovered and added to the time line, and that deliverables/activities are moved based on dependences.

## Alternatives

The sticky note approach to developing a time line is the most effective group process. A few alternatives to focusing on the entire project include having the workshop focus on a smaller segment of the project, such as:

- One stage or phase
- The work necessary to get to the next major milestone
- A stage or phase by table team so that the entire time line is developed in a phase-by-phase approach

## Recommended Debrief

After facilitating the creation of the project time line, ask:

- Is the time line complete?
- Does everyone now have a common understanding of how the project will be executed?
- Can everyone commit to this time line?

## Integration

In order to ensure that what has already been planned is consistent with the work just completed, ask:

- Does the time line support stakeholder expectations?
- Is the timing realistic given the deliverable acceptance criteria?
- Are there any procurement requirements that need to be added to the time line?
- Are there any resource constraints that impact the time line?
- Are there any key communications that need to be added to the time line?

# Defining Project Roles and Responsibilities Using the RACI Chart

PROJECT MEMBER

| DELIVERABLES | | PM. | GK. | SPONSOR | TM. | TM. | TM. |
|---|---|---|---|---|---|---|---|
| | PC | C | | A, R | | | |
| | P | R | C | I | | C | |
| | D₁ | A | I | | R | R | |
| | D₂ | A | | | R | C | R |

## Purpose

Define the roles and responsibilities for the project based on the project deliverables

## Outcome

RACI Chart

## Technique Review

A RACI chart clearly defines project roles and responsibilities for each deliverable within the project scope. Codes are used in the RACI matrix cells to document: **R**esponsible (doer of the work), **A**ccountable (ensures that the work gets done), **C**onsult (has knowledge or information that needs to be included in the creation of the deliverable), **I**nform (needs information about the status or completion of the deliverable). In a RACI table, only one person should be accountable for ensuring work gets done. An individual can have more than one letter for a deliverable and an individual does not have to have a RACI letter for every deliverable.

## Supplies

Slides to facilitate the technique, and the list of major activities/deliverables transferred into a RACI table (in Excel, Word or flip chart pages)

## Potential Slide and Sample Output

## Timing

15 – 60 minutes

## Directions

1. Review the definition of RACI.

2. Project the electronic version of the RACI on a whiteboard or screen and, as a group, go through each major activity/deliverable and agree and document who is:
   a. Accountable (A)
   b. Who is doing the work (R)
   c. Who should be consulted (C)
   d. Who should be Informed (I)

## Alternatives

1.  Focus on just the Rs and As (who is responsible and who is accountable)

2.  Instead of documenting responsibilities on a RACI chart, document them on each deliverable sticky note; for example:

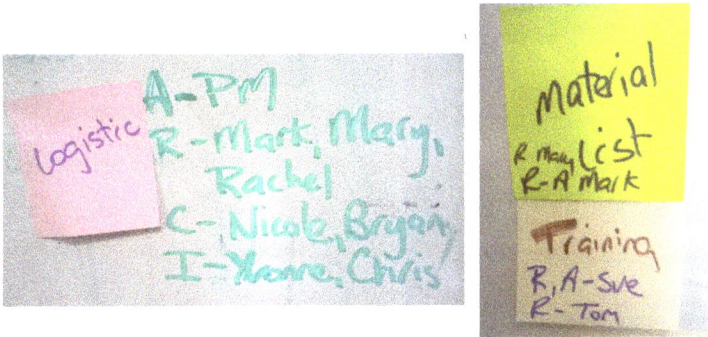

3.  Focus on specific deliverables or the just the upcoming stage/phase.

4.  Print the RACI spreadsheet out and have workshop participants, individually or at table teams, determine who has the R, A, C or I.

**Recommended Debrief**
Remind participants that their efforts provide clear accountability for the project work and then ask:
*   How will we gain commitment from those that have project responsibilities and were not in this workshop?
*   Are there any gaps between the skills we have on the team and the skills we need to complete the project work?

## Integration

In order to ensure that what has already been planned is consistent with the work just completed, ask:

- Do the required skills of the project team members impact the ability to create the deliverables or meet the acceptance criteria/requirements?
- Does the project team members' availability impact the project timing?

# Identifying, Assessing and Managing Project Risks

## Purpose
Define the project risks, assess the risks and determine how each risk should be managed

## Outcome
Project risk management plan

## Technique Review
Risk is the uncertainty that exists in all projects. Risks are the events we are aware of, but unsure if and how they may impact the project.

Risk tolerance is the acceptable level of risk in a project.

The **first step** to risk management is to identify all potential events that could impact the project. When brainstorming risks, think about uncertainty that can be related to technology, project approach, cost, timing, resources and external forces, such as regulations, vendors, competitors and environmental factors. Each of these categories can be used as a checklist to ensure that you have identified different types of potential project risks.

Risk identification can be completed at various levels of detail:
- At the project level, as a whole – to identify the uncertainty in the project alignment and approach
- At a specific project phase – to identify the uncertainty by phase
- At the deliverable or major activity level – to identify the uncertainty in individual project components

At the end of brainstorming risks, you should have an extensive list of potential events that, if they do occur, will impact the project.

Once the risks have been identified, the **second step** it to assess risks against the:
- Probability that the risk may occur.
- Impact the risk will have on the project if it does occur.

The **third step** is to create risk management strategies for each iden-tified and assessed risk. Decide if the risk should have:
- Mitigation – adding a proactive strategy or additional work designed to either reduce the risk's impact on the project or the probability of the risk occurring
- A contingency plan – a backup plan in case the risk occurs
- Both mitigation and contingency
- Neither mitigation nor contingency

Whether you apply any of the above strategies will depend on the risk assessment and the project's risk tolerance. In general,
- High risks (H's in the assessment matrixes) require both miti-gation and contingency—mitigation designed to either reduce the risk's impact on the project or the probability of the risk occurring; and a contingency plan as a backup plan in case the risk occurs and mitigation does not work.
- Medium risks (M's in the assessment matrixes) require only contingency as a backup plan in case the risk occurs. There is limited value in adding mitigation for a risk that does not have a high probability of occurrence or a high impact on the project.

- Low risks (L's in the assessment matrixes) require neither a mitigation nor contingency. Low risks have both a low probability of occurrence and a low impact if the risk does occur. Low risks should be documented and watched for just in case their probability or impact increases.

| Impact | Probability: High | Probability: Medium | Probability: Low |
|---|---|---|---|
| High | H | H | M |
| Medium | H | M | L |
| Low | M | L | L |

| Impact | Probability: High | Probability: Low |
|---|---|---|
| High | H | M |
| Low | M | L |

## Supplies

Slides to facilitate the technique, sticky notes and markers for the participants, and flip chart paper

## Potential Slide and Sample Output

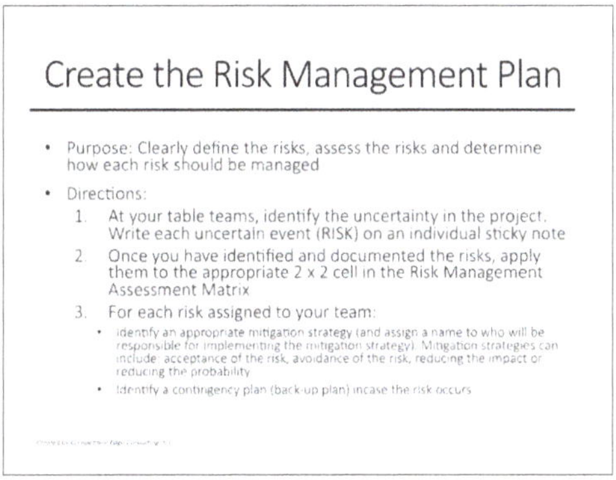
Create the Risk Management Plan
Purpose: Clearly define the risks, assess the risks and determine how each risk should be managed
Directions:
1. At your table teams, identify the uncertainty in the project. Write each uncertain event (RISK) on an individual sticky note
2. Once you have identified and documented the risks, apply them to the appropriate 2 x 2 cell in the Risk Management Assessment Matrix
3. For each risk assigned to your team:
identify an appropriate mitigation strategy (and assign a name to who will be responsible for implementing the mitigation strategy). Mitigation strategies can include: acceptance of the risk, avoidance of the risk, reducing the impact or reducing the probability
Identify a contingency plan (back-up plan) incase the risk occurs

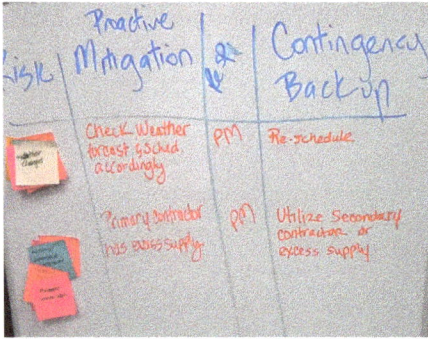 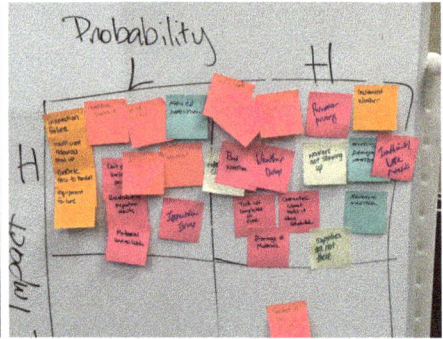

## Timing
60 minutes – 4 hours

## Directions
First, create a 2 x 2 or 3 x 3 matrix on flip chart paper and label it for probability and impact. The assignment of H (high risks), M (medium risks) and L (low risks) do not need to be included on the flip chart paper.

Before you begin the technique, review the three-step risk management process with the participants.
- Risk Identification
- Risk Assessment – against probability and impact
- Risk Management – high/high risk has mitigation and contingency, high/low and low/high have mitigation, and low/low are documented

After you've finished the review, provide the overall directions for the activity. The activity will be completed in three steps: first brainstorm and identify risks, next you will assess your risks based on probability and impact, and third, you will identify mitigation and contingency for some of the risks.

*Step One: Identification (approximately 15 minutes)*
1. Provide the following directions: At your table team, brainstorm the uncertain events that can impact the success of the

project. For each risk, document it on a sticky. Populate as many sticky notes as you can. Resist the urge to analyze and manage the risk, just document as many as you can on the sticky notes.

*Step Two: Assess (approximately 20 minutes or more)*

2. Once each table has a sufficient amount of risks identified, have them post the stickies on the 2 x 2 or 3 x 3 risk matrix.

3. Have all the participants gather near the matrix and review the risks posted in the low probability and low impact area. Remind the group that these risks will get documented, but no additional action will be taken.

4. Next, focus on the high/high risks. Ask each participant to come up and read out loud any risks they posted in the high/high category. If, during this presentation, the group determines that the item is an issue and not a risk, move it to the side to be placed on the Issue Log.

*Step Three: Manage (approximately 30 minutes or more—in a large workshop this can take several hours)*

5. Sort the high/high risks into logical categories. Possible categories include: operations, equipment, human resources, engineering, supply chain, procurement and product.

6. Have the participants split into similar groupings based on the selected categories. (Group size should be no more than six; less is better. I found teams over four participants easily move off topic.)

7. Have each group select the risks (by collecting the sticky notes) that apply to their category and return to their tables.

8. For each risk, the team will identify an appropriate mitigation strategy and assign a person who will be accountable for implementing the mitigation strategy. Remind them that mitigation strategies can include: acceptance of the risk, avoidance of the risk, reducing the impact or reducing the probability. The team will also document a contingency plan for each high/high risk in case the risk occurs.

9. Once the teams are completed with the high/high risk, have them return to the matrix and select any additional medium risks that fit in their category. For these risks, the team is to only identify contingency plans and document them on the team's flip chart.
10. Once the team work is done, have each team report out their management strategy for each risk.

## Alternatives
1. In place of identifying risks for the entire project, focus on a:
   a. Specific portion of the project
   b. Specific category of risk, like legal or financial risk
2. Identify the level of risk tolerance for the project and label the time line (see illustration) by asking the following:
   a. Where in the life of the project should the team embrace risk? Label this portion of the project "Risk Seeker."
   b. Where in the life of the project should the team minimize risks? Label this portion of the project "Risk Adverse."
3. Determine if there are risks in the Risk Adverse portion of the project that can be moved to the Risk Seeker portion of the project. This is called *front-loading risks*, doing the risky activities first so that there is either time to recover from a risk—if the risk is a show stopper and can't be managed—or cancel the project before too much effort is invested.

## Recommended Debrief

After facilitating risk management, remind participants that their work not only identifies the uncertainty in the project, but creates strategies to manage them. Before finishing this technique, ask the participants:

- Are there any risks that can be moved early in the life of the project to test them out?
- Are there any risks so high that the project should be reevaluated?

## Integration

In order to ensure that what has already been planned is consistent with the work just completed, ask if the identified risks impact the:

- Resources required?
- Project timing?

# Documenting Project Issues

## Purpose
To create an actionable log to track and resolve project issues

## Outcome
Issues and responsible individuals

## Technique Review
An issue is any event that has happened or is about to happen that will impact the project. Issues are referred to as the "known knowns"; they are the events we know that we know about. Issues are different from "known unknowns," which are the things we know we don't know about—otherwise, called risks. If this sounds confusing, it is not meant to be. Simply put, an issue has certainty and needs to be managed while risks have uncertainty (they may or may not occur, and need to be assessed).

## Supplies
Slides to facilitate the technique and flip chart paper

## Potential Slide and Sample Output

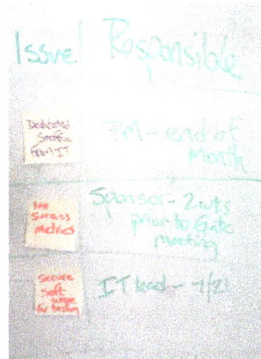

## Timing

10 minutes

## Directions

1. On a flip chart page, make three columns titled *Issue*, *Responsible* and *Targeted Completion Date*.

2. Review the issues that were identified during application of the Risk technique and any additional issues from applying the Lessons Learned technique.

3. Ask if there are any additional issues that need to be added. There may be some issues documented on the wall chart labeled: What activities provided challenges to the project that need to be avoided as the project continues (challenges)?

4. Review each Issue and identify who is responsible and when the action on the Issue Log should be completed.

## Alternatives

Have the Project Manager identify issue owners and targeted completion dates outside of the workshop.

## Recommended Debrief

To debrief this technique, ask if there are any other issues that should be added, or any questions about who is responsible for issue resolution.

## Integration

After facilitating the issue management technique, ask participants if there is any additional work that should be added to the project time line to address these issues.

# Creating the Communication Plan

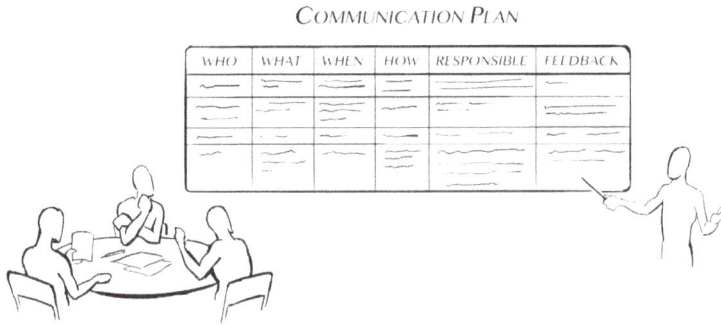

COMMUNICATION PLAN

| WHO | WHAT | WHEN | HOW | RESPONSIBLE | FEEDBACK |
|---|---|---|---|---|---|
| | | | | | |
| | | | | | |
| | | | | | |

## Purpose
To create a proactive plan for ensuring that the right people get the right information at the right time

## Outcome
Project Communication Plan

## Technique Review
Project Managers spend a significant amount of their time ensuring that everyone has a common understanding of the project's purpose, approach and progress.

The communication plan is focused on who needs information and what information they need (as opposed to what information the Project Manager thinks should be shared—just in case the Project Manager is not all-knowing). The communication plan is created by answering a series of questions and documenting them in a simple table. Actively managing communications answers the following questions:

- **Audience** –Who needs information about the project? Brainstorm all individuals that need information about the project. This list should include already identified individuals like Stakeholders and project team members, as well as anyone else inside or outside the project and organization that will need information about the project.

- **Content** – What do they need to know? For each individual, figure out what information they need. When we send unnecessary information to people, we may condition them to not read or listen to what we have to say. Make sure the information provided is audience focused. One size does not fit all. If the audience is the Sponsor, Steering Committee, Gatekeeper or other Key Stakeholders, review their success criteria (or KPIs) to see if you can provide information that is aligned with their priorities.

- **Timing** – When do they need information? Timing can be either:
  - Event driven – triggered by the arrival of an event (e.g., thirty days prior, the day of, the day after)
  - Time driven – triggered by the passage of time (e.g., every day, every week, once a month)

  Make sure the timing selected is driven by the information needs of the audience and the availability of data (no need to report costs weekly when the information is only available monthly).

- **Medium** – How will they get the information? Match the medium used to deliver the information to the audience's preferences. Don't expect everyone to have the same availability to technology that you have. There are some people that are still on non-supported versions of software (so, don't create files they cannot open), and even some that do not have cell phones (so, don't send them text messages). Again, you need to be audience focused. When developing communications, consider both a push and pull approach. Push is providing the same information in a standard way to everyone; for example, sending documentation, giving a presentation or attending a meeting to provide information. Pull is making the information available for the audience to get when they have time, or are interested in getting the information; for example, posting information to a shared drive, website or SharePoint. Remember that face to face is still the most effective medium, so use it as often as you can.

- **Responsible** – Who will provide the communication? Look at each communication individually and determine who is in the best position to share the information. Then, make them responsible. Not all project communications should come from the Project Manager. The Sponsor, Key Stakeholders and even team members can be responsible for project communications. Use the communication plan to:
  - ○ Build opportunities for team members. If a team member would like exposure to someone in the organization, then make them responsible for communicating to them, and coach them to increase their success.
  - ○ Leverage existing relationships. If a team member has a strong relationship with a Key Stakeholder, then they may be the best candidate to deliver the communication.

- **Feedback** – How will you know the communication was received as intended? Just because you told them, it does not mean that they understand the information. Look for ways to gather feedback to validate if the communication was received as intended. Some communications have feedback imbedded in the communications. For example, if you ask for an RSVP, or a decision or specific action, you can observe and see if the action occurs—validation that the message was received. Other communications will require follow-up by you to ensure that the message was received. For example, if you send out an email and then follow up with a phone call a few days later to see if there are any questions, you will find out if the email was read and if the information was understood.

## Supplies

Slides to facilitate the technique, sticky notes and markers for participants, and flip charts

## Potential Slide and Sample Output

## Timing

20 – 40 minutes

## Directions

1. Label a flip chart page *Who.* Label another flip chart page with columns titled *Who, What, When, How, Responsible* and *Feedback* (or use the column headings Audience, Content, Timing, Medium, Responsible and Feedback). Ensure that participants have access to sticky notes, markers and a flip chart.

2. Review the purpose of a Communication Plan.

3. Identify all the individuals or groups that will need information about this project. Write each individual or group on a sticky note and post them on the flip chart labeled *Who.*

4. Review the stakeholders list and add them to the Who.

5. Divide the Who sticky notes up between the workshop participants (ensure that each group has an equal amount). For each Who, have the teams identify:

a. What they need to know
b. How often they need to know it
c. How that information will get to them
d. Who is responsible for communicating this information

Ensure that this is not a duplicate of the I in the RACI chart. These communications may be at a higher level than the major activities in the RACI.

6. Let the group know that they will be sharing their Communication Plan with the entire workshop for questions and buy-in at the end of this activity.

## Alternatives
1. Focus on the communication plan for a specific project stage/ phase or upcoming decision point.

2. Identify Key Stakeholders and only create the communication plan for those selected stakeholders.

3. Have the Project Manager complete the communication plan post workshop.

4. If the project team wants to focus on internal team communication, then have each "Who/Audience" column be a project team member.

## Recommended Debrief
After facilitating this technique, have each team present their Communication Plan. Ensure that the workshop participants agree to the content of the Communication Plan.

Wrap up the communication planning by stating, "We now have proactively planned the communication in this project. With the Communication Plan and the RACI chart, this project is more likely to get the right information to the right people at the right time."

## Integration

In order to ensure that what has already been planned is consistent with the work just completed, ask if there any additional items that need to be updated—time line, risk assessment or RACI—based on the creation of the communication plan?

# Wrap-Up

## Report Out

### Purpose
Present the workshop results to the Sponsor and project leadership

### Outcome
Common understanding of the project approach

### Technique Review
There are no project management techniques used in the Report Out

### Supplies
Slides to facilitate the report out and all workshop output

### Potential Slide

Report Out

| Topic | What we Accomplished | Next Steps | What we Need From the Sponsor |
|---|---|---|---|
| Scope | | | |
| Time / Schedule | | | |
| Risks & Issues | | | |
| Communication | | | |
| Human Resources / RACI | | | |
| Costs / Financials | | | |

## Timing

15 – 60 minutes

## Directions

1. Ask for volunteers to lead the report out. Either have the Project Manager present the entire report out or have team members select specific topics to present.
2. The report out is a brief review of wall charts. If the team requires a more formal report out, create a summary slide of each technique applied to focus the team during the report out.
3. As the Facilitator, your role now is to move to the background and have the team take ownership of what they have created. Going forward, it is their project, their plan. Your role is almost complete.

## Alternatives

If leadership is not available for the report out at the end of the workshop, here are two options:

1. Have them call in using a video tool so that they can see and hear the report out content.

2. Hold a meeting or phone call at the earliest time available. Capture photos of the team during the workshop and of the wall charts—this will provide a more complete understanding of the workshop outcome than reading through project documentation that is created from the workshop wall charts.

## Recommended Debrief

After the Report Out is completed, thank everyone for the contribution to developing the Project Plan and thank the leaders for returning for the Report Out. Ask if there are any questions before we close out the workshop.

## Integration

There is no integration needed for this portion of the workshop.

# Workshop Close Out

### Purpose
Close out the workshop and thank everyone for the collaboration

### Outcome
Closure to the workshop

### Technique Review
There are no project management techniques used in the Workshop Close Out

### Supplies
Slides to facilitate the close out

### Potential Slide

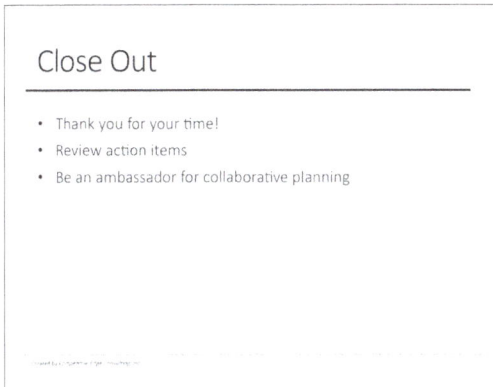

Close Out

- Thank you for your time!
- Review action items
- Be an ambassador for collaborative planning

### Timing
15 – 60 minutes

### Directions
1. Review the closing slide and ask each participant to share their answers to the following questions. As a result of this workshop:

    a.   What do you think?

    b.   What will you do?

    c.   What will you say?

2.   Thank the participants for their hard work and contributions to the workshop.

3.   Create an action plan of any activities that need to be completed post workshop. Make sure that there are names and dates next to each activity. The action plan belongs to the Project Manager, not the meeting Facilitator.

4.   Make sure the team collects the wall charts—they are the team's documentation of the project approach.

5.   If you have a scribe that is capturing the wall chart content electronically, determine and commit to when the electronic documents will be forwarded to the Project Manager.

### Recommended Debrief

After the Close Out is completed, thank everyone for the contribution and verify that any action items or next steps are clearly defined.

### Integration

There is no integration needed for this portion of the workshop.

# Section 4:
# POST WORKSHOP

This section provides details on the work to be completed after the workshop is over.

# Updating Documentation

Once the workshop is over, there is still work to do. If you have the luxury of a scribe during the workshop, then information may be captured as it is created and the documentation will is complete. If you are working without a scribe, or not all information could be captured, then you will need to gather the data generated during the workshop to create the project documentation. When transporting wall charts, take into consideration the following:

- Make sure all wall charts are labeled—if there is more than one chart for a technique, label and number each chart.
- Take photographs of all the wall charts.
- Tape any sticky notes to the flip chart pages before rolling the charts up. Sometimes the sticky notes will stick to the back side of another page and it could be hard to determine which chart they belong to if they are needed for reference.

Project documentation can take many forms. Some projects have access to a project team room where the wall charts can hang for anyone to see and update. Some organizations are satisfied with photographs of the wall charts that can be shared electronically. Some organizations will have documentation standards that will require transcribing the charts into electronic forms/templates in the form of a Project Plan.

A Project Plan may contain:

- Business Need
- Scope

- o Objective
- o Deliverable and Acceptance Criteria
- o Assumptions/Constraints
- Risk
- Roles and Responsibilities
- Schedule
- Financials
- Stakeholder Management Plan
- Communication Plan

Make sure that documentation from the workshop is available to all workshop participants and others as appropriate.

# Completing Action Items

Every workshop will end with a list of items that need to be completed. Make sure that during the workshop someone is capturing action items and assigning clear responsibility to each item. Common action items include:

- Sharing workshop outcomes and decisions with non-workshop participants

- Validating RACI charts with non-workshop participants whose names are identified as Responsible or Accountable for work in the project

- Re-evaluating project staffing

- Re-evaluating project funding

- Meetings to facilitate discussion about other work that the project impacts or is dependent on

- Alternative approaches that could reduce the project timing, modify resource requirements or impact project risks

# Post Workshop Roles and Responsibilities

In addition to action items that are identified during the workshop, everyone has responsibilities after the workshop. Here is a list of responsibilities by role for post-workshop activities:

| Role | Responsibilities in Workshop |
|---|---|
| **Sponsor** | • Review workshop outcomes<br>• Ensure resource availability for post-workshop activities<br>• Follow up with ongoing support for workshop output |
| **Project Manager** | • Take ownership of workshop materials—taking photos of all flip charts and then gathering all workshop documentation<br>• Talk with the Scribe to get electronic copies of items captured during the workshop<br>• Follow up on next steps<br>• Summarize and communicate the workshop output to those who were not at the workshop but need to understand the Project Plan and decisions made |

| Role | Responsibilities in Workshop |
|---|---|
| **Facilitator** | • Follow up with the Sponsor and Project Manager to assess their satisfaction with the workshop<br>• Reflect on your personal learning from facilitating the workshop and incorporate these learnings into your next workshop<br>• Send a thank you to the Sponsor and Project Manager for their involvement in the workshop success<br>• Follow up with the Scribe regarding capturing and turnover of electronic documentation |
| **Participants** | • Complete any action items<br>• Communicate the value of the workshop to non-participants |
| **Scribe** | • Complete any action items<br>• Communicate the value of the workshop to non-participants |

# Resources for Supporting Workshops

For additional resources to support your application of project management, visit our website: www.cectraining.com. At the website, you will find:

- Planning forms for workshops
- Whitepaper on leadership research on the behaviors needed to be successful for program and project managers
- Worksheets to access how project management is being applied on a project
- Template for WBS in Excel and Microsoft Project that include the project management activities needed for initiation, planning, execution, control and closing stages
- Templates for Project Plans and Project Charters
- A link to *The Practitioner's Guide to Project Management* that provides simple, effective techniques in a way that encourages collaborative conversations with key resources and delivers business value. This book contains:
  - Foundational techniques – the value they provide and the questions they help answer
  - Roles and responsibility clarity for key project players across the life of a project

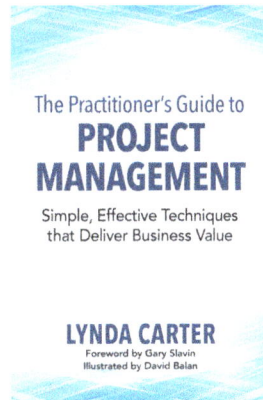

The Practitioner's Guide to
**PROJECT MANAGEMENT**
Simple, Effective Techniques
that Deliver Business Value

**LYNDA CARTER**
Foreword by Gary Slavin
Illustrated by David Balan

- ○ Explanation of project management deliverables – their purpose, content and tips on how to create them
- ○ Answers to common questions about applying project management techniques

If you have questions or would like to share your ideas, reach out to us on the Contact Us page. We would love to hear from you.

# APPENDIXES

The appendixes contain a quick reference of: planning and closing forms, participant invitations, potential slides for facilitating a workshop, and photos of sample output.

# Appendix A: Planning and Closing Forms

Use these forms as a worksheet to assist in your workshop planning. You can recreate these forms and modify them to meet your needs.

## Planning Worksheet

Project: _____

Sponsor: _____

Project Manager: _____

| | |
|---|---|
| Workshop Purpose: | |
| Desired Workshop Duration: | |

| Project Management Techniques | Completed in Workshop | Created Prior to Workshop and Reviewed in Workshop | NOT included in Workshop |
|---|---|---|---|
| Project Goal | ○ | ○ | ○ |
| Lessons Learned | ○ | ○ | ○ |
| Stakeholders (KPI) | ○ | ○ | ○ |
| Deliverables | ○ | ○ | ○ |
| Deliverable Requirements | ○ | ○ | ○ |
| Time Line | ○ | ○ | ○ |
| Roles and Responsibilities (RACI) | ○ | ○ | ○ |
| Risks | ○ | ○ | ○ |
| Issues | ○ | ○ | ○ |
| Communication Plan | ○ | ○ | ○ |
| Other | ○ | ○ | ○ |

How will workshop output be captured post-workshop? And by whom?

Who will kick off the Workshop? What will they present?

Who will be in attendance at the report out? What are their expectations?

Who should be included as workshop participants?

| |
|---|
| Are there any knowledge gaps? |
| What risks might exist that will impact the success of the Workshop? |
| Who do you need to meet with to gather additional information so that the Workshop agenda can be drafted? |

## Closing Worksheet

| |
|---|
| 1. Who should be involved in sharing project learnings? |
| 2. What is the original value promised in a Business Case or Project Charter? |
| 3. What are the current project baselines for: goal, deliverables, requirements, timing, budget and resources? |
| 4. What data should be gathered:<br>a. Project actuals?<br>b. Survey of project team?<br>c. Survey of stakeholder satisfaction? |

5.  How will lessons learned be shared with other projects and stakeholders?

6.  What happens with unrealized goals/objectives, and how will outstanding issues or concerns be handled?

7.  How will celebrating the project success be incorporated into the closing workshop?

# Appendix B: Participant Invitations

It is critical to get the right people in the room to kick off and plan the project/program. If participants are missing, project components could be omitted and buy-in is incomplete.

Here is a simple calendar notification or email:

Save the Date. Your participation is required/requested in a planning workshop for Project _____ (project name) on xx/xx/xxxx. Details to follow.

Here is a draft of an invitation. Feel free to modify it and use it for your workshops.

Subject: Project _____ (project name) Planning Workshop

A Project Plan is being created for the _____ (project name) project. In order to create a comprehensive Project Plan, your presence is required/requested. This project has full support of management.

The purpose of the workshop is _____.

Other individuals participating in the workshop include: _____ (this can include a list of names or names and functional areas represented)

The workshop will be held at _____
(workshop location, if the workshop is off-site, include
the location address, parking or any other related
logistics).

The agenda is (I rarely put timing on the agenda shared
in an invitation except the start and end times):

| Topic | Details |
|---|---|
| 8:00 am Kick-off | Workshop purpose, agenda review, introductions and expectations, confirming the project goal |
| Stakeholder Expectations | Establishing project success criteria by key stakeholder |
| Deliverables by Phase | Defining success for each project phase and defining the major activities and final deliverables by phase |
| Time Line | Creating the project time line |
| Responsibility by Deliverable | Identifying Responsible and Accountable resources for each major activity/deliverable |
| Lunch | |
| Begin Detailing the WBS | Selecting one deliverable from each functional area and documenting the requirements for each deliverable as well as the work necessary to create the deliverable |
| Project Risks | Identifying project risks and determining risk strategies, defining and integrating mitigation strategies into the project time line |
| Close Out 4:30pm | Determine next steps and action items |

The workshop will be a working session. Plan to be engaged for the entire session. The workshop starts promptly at _____ (time) and runs until _____ (time). Let the Project Manager know if you need assistance in rescheduling other events.

I look forward to your active participation in planning this project,

Senior Manager, VP (Signature of Project Sponsor)

# Appendix C: Potential Slides

Having slides to facilitate the workshop provides visual directions and a reference point for the participants. Usually, projecting the slides is sufficient, but in some workshops, copies of the slides are provided to the participants. Feel free to reproduce and modify these slides for your workshop.

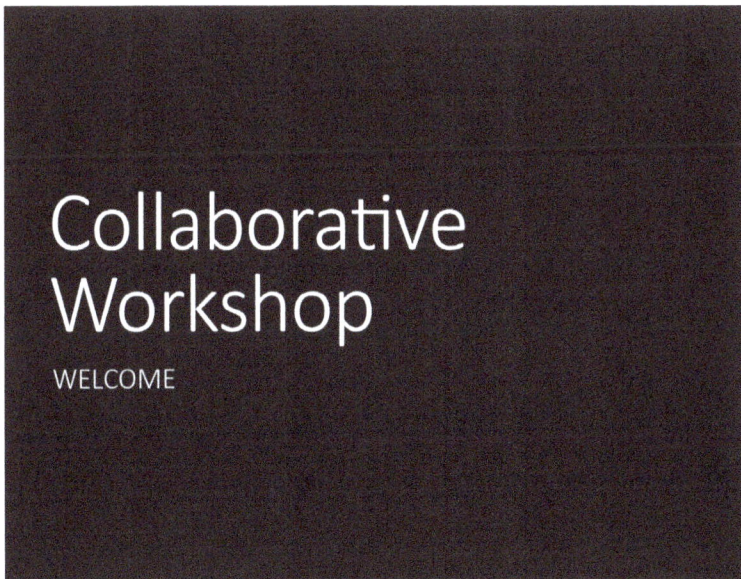

Collaborative Workshop
WELCOME

## Agenda

| Estimated Timing | Topics |
|---|---|
| 8:00 – 9:30 | Sponsor Kick-off, Introductions, Ground Rules & Expectations |
| 9:30 – 9:45 | Break |
| 9:45 – 10:15 | Lessons Learned |
| 10:15 – 11:00 | Stakeholders |
| 11:00 – 12:00 | Deliverables & Time Line |
| 12:00 – 1:00 | Lunch |
| 1:00 – 2:30 | Risk & Issues |
| 2:30 – 2:45 | Break |
| 2:45 – 3:00 | RACI |
| 3:00 – 3:30 | Communications |
| 3:30 – 4:00 | Financials |
| 4:00 – 4:15 | Report out Preparation |
| 4:15 – 5:00 | Report out to Sponsor |

Created by *Competitive Edge Consulting, Inc.*

## Purpose

- Purpose: Develop a project plan to achieve the project goal
- Output:
  - Working Project Plan for the project including: stakeholder assessment, goals, deliverables, time line, risks, issues, responsibilities, communication plan and estimated financials
  - Report out to our Sponsor
- Excluding: list any items, that need to be identified, that will not be included in the workshop

Created by *Competitive Edge Consulting, Inc.*

# Beginning with the End in Mind

- What we will report out to the Sponsor at the end of the workshop:

| Topic | What we Accomplished | Next Steps | Support Needed |
|---|---|---|---|
| Stakeholder assessment | | | |
| Scope: goals & deliverables | | | |
| Time / Schedule | | | |
| Risks & Issues | | | |
| Costs / Financials | | | |
| Human Resources / RACI | | | |
| Communications | | | |

Created by Competitive Edge Consulting, Inc.

# Ground Rules

- Be fully engaged
- No phones
- No computers
- Be open to new ideas and different perspectives
- Take ownership of the workshop output

Created by Competitive Edge Consulting, Inc.

# Introductions

- Name
- Role
- How you can contribute to the success of this project

Created by *Competitive Edge Consulting, Inc.*

# Kick-off

- A word from our Sponsor:
  - Project Background
    - *Na oiaoiif s ijreroirodl   jpd a'*
    - *A ajfaid*
    - *Asl iijf gjitti ad' jma't riij mtjuptg gs gri gj oti s gyupet*

Created by *Competitive Edge Consulting, Inc.*

# Project History

- What has happened to date on the project
- Project SMART goal – if one has been established
- Project constraints – desired due date, requirements, budget. . .

# Defining the Goal

- Now that we have a common understanding of the project's purpose, let's clarify the project goal using the SMART criteria:
  - Specific
  - Measurable
  - Actionable
  - Realistic
  - Time-bound
- In teams, and in your own words, define the goal of the project in a single simple sentence
- Document your goal statement on the flip chart

## Revisiting the Goal

- Now that we have a common vision of the project, let's confirm the project goal
- In teams, and in your own words, define the goal of the project in a single simple sentence
- Document your goal statement on the flip chart

Created by *Competitive Edge Consulting, Inc.*

## Lessons Learned

- Purpose: To share learning from past projects that celebrates what was done well so that it can be repeated and identify what has not gone well so that it can be avoided
- Directions:
  1. Answer the following questions and document your answer on individual sticky notes:
     - What activities provided challenges to past projects, that need to be avoided?
     - What activities provided value that should be continued?
  2. Post your sticky notes on the labeled flip charts

Created by *Competitive Edge Consulting, Inc.*

# Defining Stakeholders

- Purpose: To identify key stakeholders and what is critical to success from their perspective

- Directions:
    1. Identify key stakeholders, write each stakeholder on a sticky note
    2. Place the stakeholder on the Prioritization Chart
    3. For your assigned stakeholders:
        - *Discuss what their interests and concerns may be*
        - *Define their success metrics*

# Define the Deliverables

- Purpose: Identify project deliverables: final, interim and project management

- Directions:
    1. Identify the deliverables and major activities that need to be completed during the project
    2. Document each major activity or deliverable on a sticky note
    3. The sticky notes will be used to build the project time line

# Acceptance Criteria

- Purpose: Provide clarity to what each project deliverable will contain in order for the deliverable to be acceptable
- Directions:
    1. Review your assigned deliverable
    2. Determine and document the criteria that will be used to evaluate the quality of this deliverable
    3. Prioritize the list by identifying acceptance criteria that:
        - Must be included for the deliverable to be usable
        - Should be included in the deliverable
        - Could be included if there is time and resources available (these are nice to have items)

Created by *Competitive Edge Consulting, Inc.*

# Create the Schedule

- Purpose: Create a deliverable-based time line, collaboratively

- Directions:
    1. Using the major activities or deliverables previously documented on a sticky note, apply them to the time line (placing them either where the activity should begin or end)
    2. After all activities are posted, the time line will be reviewed as a group

Created by *Competitive Edge Consulting, Inc.*

# Create the RACI

- Purpose: Clearly define the roles and responsibilities of the project based on the major activities and deliverables identified in the schedule
- Directions: For each deliverable identified on the project schedule, determine who is:
  - *Accountable – ensures the work gets done*
  - *Responsible – doer of the work*
  - *Consult – have input to the work*
  - *Informed – will be updated as to work progress and completion*

Created by *Competitive Edge Consulting, Inc.*

# Create the Risk Management Plan

- Purpose: Clearly define the risks, assess the risks and determine how each risk should be managed
- Directions:
  1. At your table teams, identify the uncertainty in the project. Write each uncertain event (RISK) on an individual sticky note
  2. Once you have identified and documented the risks, apply them to the appropriate 2 x 2 cell in the Risk Management Assessment Matrix
  3. For each risk assigned to your team:
     - Identify an appropriate mitigation strategy (and assign a name to who will be responsible for implementing the mitigation strategy). Mitigation strategies can include: acceptance of the risk, avoidance of the risk, reducing the impact or reducing the probability
     - Identify a contingency plan (back-up plan) incase the risk occurs

Created by *Competitive Edge Consulting, Inc.*

# Create the Issue Log

- Purpose: Create an actionable Issue Log to track and resolve project issues
- Directions: For each issues documented, identify:
  - *An individual who is accountable*
  - *Timing for when action will be taken*

# Create the Communication Plan

- Purpose: Clearly define the communication needed so that the right people get the right information at the right time
- Directions:
  1. Identify all potential audiences for communication, document each audience on a sticky note
  2. Bring your audience sticky notes to the wall chart
  3. For your assigned audience, determine their:
     - Information Requirement
     - Frequency
     - Medium
     - Who is Responsible

## Report Out

| Topic | What we Accomplished | Next Steps | What we Need From the Sponsor |
|---|---|---|---|
| Scope | | | |
| Time / Schedule | | | |
| Risks & Issues | | | |
| Communication | | | |
| Human Resources / RACI | | | |
| Costs / Financials | | | |

Created by *Competitive Edge Consulting, Inc.*

## Close Out

- Thank you for your time!
- Review action items
- Be an ambassador for collaborative planning

Created by *Competitive Edge Consulting, Inc.*

# Appendix D: Sample Workshop Output

A visual of what the participants are trying to create can be helpful. Don't limit yourself to the output samples that are provided here. Use these photos to help you guide the teams to create simple documentation of their project decisions.

## Lessons Learned

## Stakeholder Identification and Assessment

## Stakeholder Management Plan

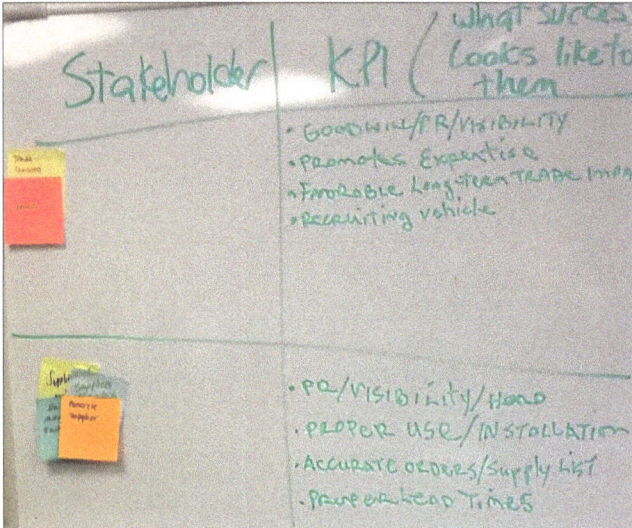

## Project Deliverables

## Acceptance Criteria

## Project Time Line

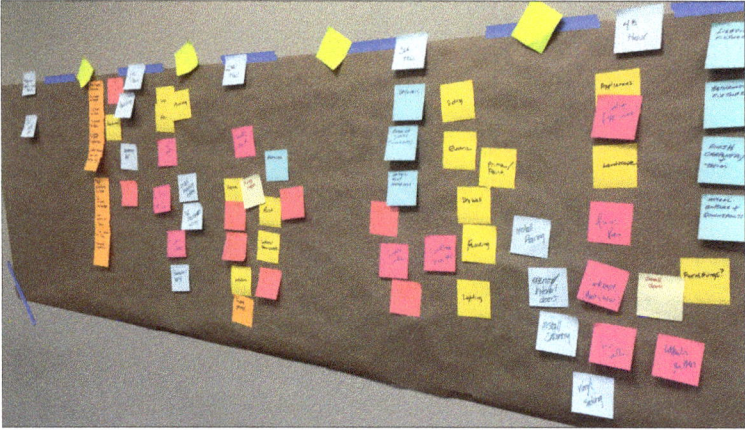

## Traditional RACI Chart

## RACI Documented Next to the Deliverable Sticky Note

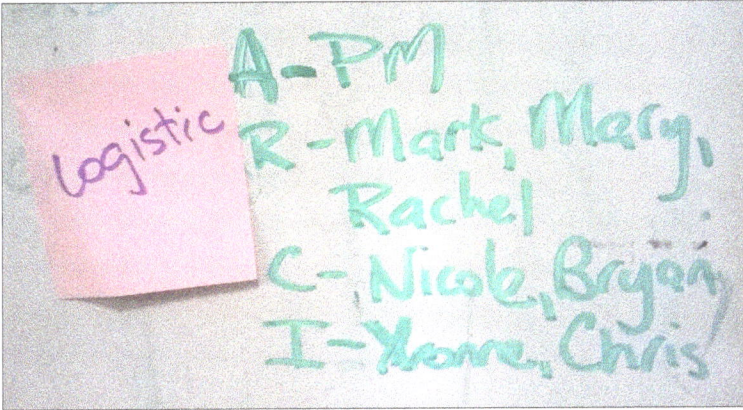

## RACI Documented on the Deliverables Sticky Note

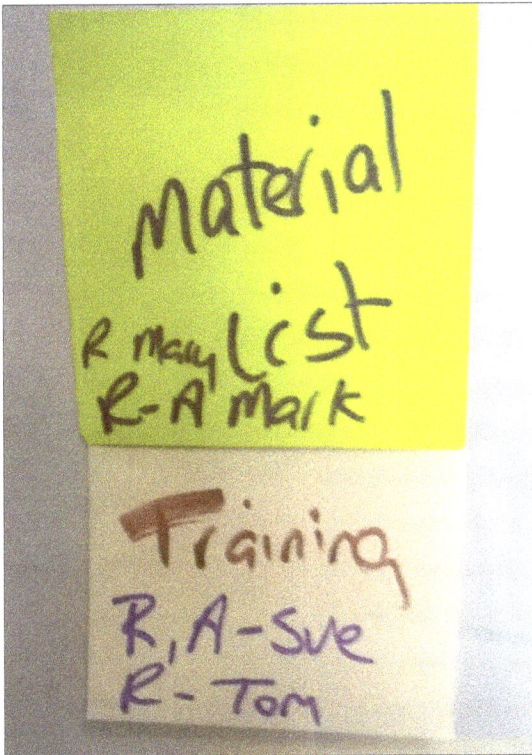

## Risk Identification and Assessment (using the 2x2 matrix)

## Risk Management Strategies

## Project Issues

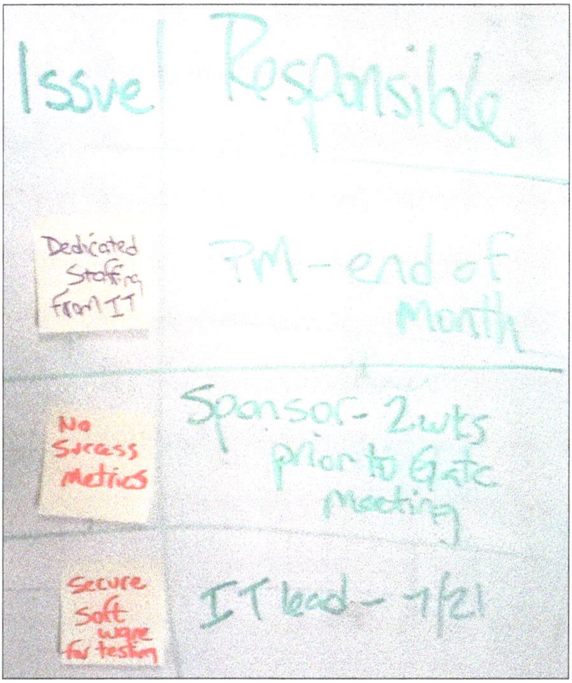


## Communication Plan

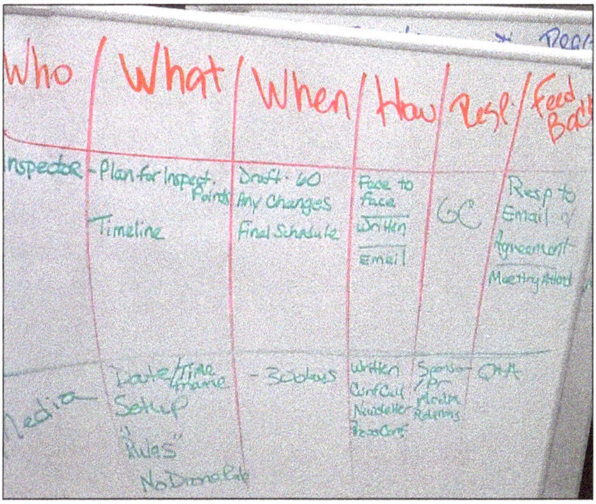

# GLOSSARY

This glossary focuses on key terms related to project management as well as other terms and abbreviations used within the text of this book.

**aka.** An abbreviation for *also known as*.

**Business Case.** The business justification for a project.

**buffer.** See **contingency.**

**Capability Maturity Model Integration (CMMI).** Software Engineering Institute's model that provides a standard for which many processes can be assessed.

**change.** See **scope change**.

**Change Log.** The log that is used to track requested changes (often referred to as scope change) to the project once the Project Plan has been approved.

**Closing.** The final step (phase or stage) of a project that is used to capture project learning and improve the strategies used in future projects.

**CMMI.** An abbreviation for *Capability Maturity Model Integration*. See also **Capability Maturity Model Integration (CMMI)**.

**contingency.** Also called *buffer* or *safety*. The additional time or money in a project used to absorb the things you did not know you did not know about (sometimes called the "unknown unknowns").

**critical path.** The longest chain of work sequenced by dependences.

**Decomposition Diagram.** See **Work Breakdown Structure (WBS)**.

**deliverables.** Something tangible that is created as a result of the project. See also **project deliverables** and **project management deliverables**.

**duration.** The total time to complete the work, taking into consideration the effort, calendar days plus the availability of resources (e.g., eight hours of effort for a person who is working only 20 percent of the time on the project will take a duration of five days).

**Earned Value or Earned Value Management (EVM).** A standard set of equations used to determine project status at a point in time and create projections of project completion.

**effort.** The amount of time it takes to complete the work without the consideration of the calendar.

**EVM.** An abbreviation for *Earned Value Management*. See also **Earned Value or Earned Value Management (EVM)**.

**Execution.** The third step (stage or phase) of a project—when the project work is done.

**float.** Also called *slack*. The work items or deliverables that are not on the critical path.

**Gantt chart.** The graphical representation of a project schedule that displays deliverables or major blocks of work across time.

**Gatekeeper.** A project decision maker.

**Initiation.** The first step (phase or stage) of a project that is used to clarify what the idea is, and develop a high-level best guess of what work, resources and time it will take to bring the idea to reality.

**issue.** Any event that has happened or is about to happen that will impact the project. Issues are referred to as the "known knowns."

**Issue Log.** The log that is used to track events that occur and require action during project execution.

**IT.** An abbreviation for *information technology*.

**Key Performance Indicator (KPI).** A specific expectation or success criteria for the outcome of a project.

**Key Stakeholder.** The high-priority stakeholders—the ones that usually have more interest in the project execution or project outcome, more influence on the work being done, and/or more power and authority within the organization. See also **Stakeholder**.

**KPI.** An abbreviation for *Key Performance Indicator*. See also **Key Performance Indicator**.

**Lessons Learned.** The document that captures the knowledge acquired during the project from the perspectives of the Sponsor, Stakeholders, Project Manager and project team members.

**milestone.** A point in time on a project schedule that indicates when a specific event will occur.

**MoSCoW.** The technique for prioritizing requirements into: must have, should have, could have and won't have.

**Network Diagram.** Also called *Program Evaluation Review Technique (PERT)*. A visual display of either project deliverables or project work organized by finish-to-start dependency.

**PERT.** An abbreviation for *Program Evaluation Review Technique.* See also **Network Diagram**.

**Planning.** The second step (phase or stage) of a project that is used to create the detailed strategy needed to achieve the approved project goals.

**PMBOK.** An abbreviation for *Project Management Body of Knowledge.* See also ***Project Management Body of Knowledge (PMBOK)***.

**PMI.** An abbreviation for *Project Management Institute.*

**PMO.** An abbreviation for *Project (or Program) Management Office.* See also **Project (or Program) Management Office**.

**Program Evaluation Review Technique (PERT).** See **Network Diagram.**

**project.** Something new or something unique that needs to get done.

**Project Charter.** A project management deliverable that documents the common understanding of a project need and high-level project strategy. See also **project management deliverables**.

**project deliverables.** Items created to achieve the project goals. See also **project management deliverables**.

**Project Evaluation.** A project management deliverable that provides an overall summary of the project, assesses the project's actual performance versus the planned performance, and highlights key improvements that can be leveraged for future projects.

**project management.** Standardized tools and techniques that increase the likelihood a project will be planned and executed successfully.

***Project Management Body of Knowledge (PMBOK).*** The standard for project management, published by Project Management Institute.

**project management deliverables.** Items created for the management of a formal project. See also **project deliverables**.

**project management maturity.** An assessment within an organization that measures the acceptance and use of a standardized project management process.

**Project Manager.** The person responsible for facilitating the project planning, execution and closing while providing leadership to the project team.

**Project (or Program) Management Office.** A function within an organization that is dedicated to the support of project management.

**Project Plan.** Also called *Statement of Work (SOW)*. An evergreen project management deliverable that contains a detailed project strategy.

**project team.** The personnel who support the Project Manager and complete the project work.

**R&D.** An abbreviation for *research and development*.

**RACI.** A chart that is used to define project responsibilities by deliverable: Responsible (doer of the work), Accountable (ensures that the work gets done), Consult (has knowledge or information that needs to be included in the creation of the deliverable), Inform (needs information about the status or completion of the deliverable).

**requirements.** The expectations of the project, which are often defined in terms of features, functions or value delivered.

**residual risk.** The amount of remaining risk after high risks have been mitigated.

**risk.** The uncertainty that could impact the outcome of a project.

**risk reserve.** A buffer of time and money held in reserve to absorb a portion of the risk contingency if the risk occurs and the contingency plan needs to be executed.

**risk tolerance.** The amount of risk that is appropriate for the project.

**risk trigger.** An early indicator that a risk is about to occur.

**ROI.** An abbreviation for *return on investment*.

**ROM.** An abbreviation for *Rough Order of Magnitude*. See also **Rough Order of Magnitude (ROM)**.

**Rough Order of Magnitude (ROM).** A high-level estimate that is used to determine the amount of effort and duration required for a project.

**safety.** See **contingency**.

**scope.** The term used to define what will and will not be included in the project; scope includes: goals, deliverables, quality and work.

**scope change.** Any modification to the scope that is documented and agreed to in the approved Project Plan.

**SDLC.** An abbreviation for *software development lifecycle*.

**SEI.** An abbreviation for *Software Engineering Institute*.

**slack.** See **float**.

**SME.** An abbreviation for *Subject Matter Expert*. See also **Subject Matter Expert (SME)**.

**SOW.** An abbreviation for *Statement of Work*. See also **Project Plan**.

**Sponsor.** The person who represents the primary project benefactor and sets the overall project direction.

**Stakeholder.** Anyone who is actively involved in the project, or impacted by the execution or completion of the project. See also **Key Stakeholder**.

**Statement of Work (SOW).** See **Project Plan**.

**Steering Committee.** A team that provides a cross-functional perspective and overall support for project planning and execution.

**Subject Matter Expert (SME).** The person who provides expertise on project strategy and project-related information.

**WBS.** An abbreviation for *Work Breakdown Structure*. See also **Work Breakdown Structure (WBS)**.

**Work Breakdown Structure (WBS).** A project management term used to reference breaking all the project work down in a hierarchical and structured or organized manner.

**Work Package.** A bundle of work that, once completed, creates a completed deliverable or portion of a deliverable.

**workshop.** A collaborative working meeting held for the purpose of creating a common vision and strategy to achieve the project goal.

www.ingramcontent.com/pod-product-compliance
Lightning Source LLC
Chambersburg PA
CBHW042311210326
41598CB00041B/7345